A Household Word

A Household Word

Carol Band

Author of the award-winning humor column,
"A Household Word"

iUniverse, Inc.
New York Bloomington Shanghai

A Household Word

iUniverse books may be ordered through booksellers or by contacting:

iUniverse
1663 Liberty Drive
Bloomington, IN 47403
www.iuniverse.com
1-800-Authors (1-800-288-4677)

Some of these columns were previously published by United Parenting Publications as *A Household Word*.

ISBN: 978-0-595-44982-8 (pbk)
ISBN: 978-0-595-89301-0 (ebk)

Printed in the United States of America

Contents

A Note from the Author

I'd like to say that I wrote this book because I am a parenting expert and want to share the secrets of raising smart, successful, well-adjusted kids. The truth is, I'm not an expert and, while my kids are okay, I can't take any credit or blame. They could just as easily have become axe murders or pole dancers. And frankly, there's still time.

Carol Band

1

Afterbirth

A Household Word: **Brunch**

Brunch is created by combining breakfast and lunch, adding champagne and jazz music and subtracting children. Not happening.

RUNNING ON KID TIME

I recently celebrated my birthday and my oldest son (sweet boy) gave me a t-shirt that says, *In Dog Years, I'm Dead*. Nice. "Ha! "You are over 300 years old!" my youngest figured with a rare burst of mathematical insight. Then he eyed the dog. "That means Chester is twenty-one … Wahooo! Go Chetty! You can buy beer!" Nice.

Although I seem to have a grasp of how canine time is calculated (after all, multiplying by seven, while not as easy as multiplying by five, is still fairly straightforward), I haven't been able to comprehend what makes my kids tick. The struggle for us to synchronize is a daily effort. Maybe that's because my children aren't living on Eastern Standard, Central, Mountain or Pacific Time. They're on Kid Time.

If you set your clock to Kid Time, an hour of TV isn't nearly enough, nine o'clock is way too early for bed and Saturday morning, while your parents are still sleeping, is the perfect time to try to cut your own bangs. On the kid calendar, Christmas is always too far away, summer vacation lasts forever, and your birthday is a national holiday. If you ask my kids, they'll check their watches and tell you that recess is too short, math class is too long, and all teachers are all really, really old. Even older than me.

In Kid Time, sitting through an hour-long church service is equivalent to being stranded on a rock in the middle of the ocean for a month. You are hungry. You are starving. "Mom, do you have any Tic Tacs? When will they pass out the little pieces of bread? I'm hungry, I'm thirsty. Will there be donuts at coffee hour? I am getting weaker … I am fading away … I am slipping under the pews … Ahhhh…."

Likewise, a twelve-year-old boy who is supposed to practice the piano for thirty minutes will race through his piece and declare, "I'm done!" after a minute and a half. That's because a half hour of practicing the piano in Kid Time is like an adult spending three hours at a Weird Al Yankovich concert. It is interminable. Maybe we should try to be more understanding.

As parents, perhaps we should learn to expect a different kind of punctuality from our kids. For instance, when an adult says, "Do your homework right now," a child will say, "Okay," but she will not move. That's because in Adult Time, "right now" means sometime soon, like in the next few minutes. But in Kid Time, "right now" means not until your mother has asked you again and again and again, and then not until she finally stomps into the den, snaps off the television and says, "I said *Right. Now!*" I try to accommodate the members of my own household who are operating on Kid Time, but it's not easy.

"Can you take me to Shawn's house?" my son asked at eight o'clock on Saturday morning.

"Soon," I said. For me, "soon" means later—after I've had a cup of coffee, after I've changed out of my pajamas and after Shawn's parents are conscious.

For my son, Lewis, who apparently has no snooze button on his kid clock, "soon" means now. Right now. "Are you ready yet? Can we go now? How about now?"

My oldest son also has a clock that runs on its own sweet time.

"Take out the garbage," I say.

"I am," he replies, even though I can see him sitting barefoot at the kitchen table consuming vast quantities of expensive, not-from-concentrate orange juice. Again, the fact that I am able to see him is not because he is able to bend the time space continuum. It's because he is on Kid Time where "I am" means he will … eventually. Maybe.

Kid Time starts the second you become a parent and, apparently, just keeps on ticking. Anyone who has ever walked the floor with a colicky newborn, sent a teenage driver out with the family car, waited in an emergency room with a toddler or read *Green Eggs and Ham* over and over and over knows that time with kids can make minutes seem like an eternity and the years pass in a moment. Even dog years.

PHOTO OPPORTUNITY

We've all seen the photos of bad celebrity parents. Michael Jackson dangled his newborn son over a balcony. Britney Spears drove with her four-month-old on her lap and the late crocodile hunter, Steve Irwin, held his baby daughter in one hand and fed raw chicken to a gigantic croc with the other. Shudder.

All of these stories make me feel pretty darn smug about my own parenting skills. Of course, I don't have the paparazzi following me around twenty-four-seven. Good thing, because if I did, I'm pretty sure that my kids would be wards of the state. Not that I'm a bad mother, but I have had a few mommy moments that are probably better left undocumented.

Two weeks before my due date, I went to my cousin's wedding. The best man offered up a toast and I took a sip (okay, maybe two) of champagne. I had been alcohol, aspirin, and caffeine-free throughout my pregnancy. I only ate organic food and made my husband change the litter box, pump the gasoline and do the heavy lifting. I avoided saunas, secondhand smoke and sushi. I stopped dying my hair! I was a saint and I was eight-and-a-half months pregnant. The baby already had its fingers and toes and probably most of its brain cells. I didn't want to insult the bride and groom by not raising my glass and wishing them well, and I knew that having a few sips of champagne couldn't hurt. But, if the photogs from the tabloids had been there, they would have shot a close-up of me with the glass to my lips and the headlines would have announced *Band and Baby Booze it Up!*

Once I gave birth, the photo opportunities increased. Once (okay, maybe two or three times), my daughter fell asleep in her car seat on the way home from the grocery store. Rather than wake her up to bring her inside, I parked in the driveway, cracked the windows and let her finish her nap in the minivan. I could watch her from the living room window and run to the car the minute she woke up. Still, if the paparazzi had been lurking behind the garage, the caption accompanying the photo of my kid crying in the car would have read: *Band Abandons Baby in Backseat!*

I continue to provide fodder for the tabloids. If only they were paying attention! I sent my oldest son to his first day of kindergarten with a full-blown case of the chicken pox ... *A Pox on Band!* And when my daughter broke her finger, I thought she was being dramatic, so I didn't take her to the doctor for two days ... *Band Gives Doc the Finger!* This week alone, I neglected to pack my son a bag lunch for a school field trip ... *Band Starves Son!* and completely missed the deadline to sign up for fall soccer ... *Band Drops the Ball!*

When it comes to parenting, I'm not perfect. Fortunately, there aren't any pictures to prove it.

FORECAST: SHOWERS UNLIKELY

Yesterday, my son needed a baby picture of himself to bring to school. He's a third child, so we don't have any. Instead, I dug out one of the millions of baby photos of his older brother. (Hey, all babies look alike). But lately I've been worried that the money that I've saved on film processing may have to be used for my youngest child's therapy. I worry that being a third kid—my third kid—might be psychologically scarring.

When I was pregnant with my first child, I expected the world to sit up and take notice and it did. My pregnancy was a novelty. Friends patted my belly and asked me if I planned to breastfeed. Co-workers waged bets on my due date, and my mother-in-law hosted a baby shower that netted an umbrella stroller and enough booties to outfit a team of sled dogs.

But, when I was pregnant with my third kid, nobody really noticed. I was just pregnant … again. Strangers in the supermarket eyed my two kids already in tow and felt free to lecture me on the evils of overpopulation. Nobody threw me a baby shower. Everybody thought that since all the furniture in my living room was made by Fisher-Price that I must not need any more baby stuff. But they were wrong.

By the time my third kid came along, all the bibs were stained, all the picture books were ripped and the umbrella stroller had been converted into a go-cart. The childhood of my third-born has been a vastly different experience than that of my first two kids. Let's take a look:

The first child: Had a bureau bulging with stacks of tiny sailor suits and dry-clean-only sweaters that were worn just for photos.

The second child: Wore only pink. (After two years of primary colors and T-shirts with trucks appliqués, Grandma was itching to buy pink.)

The third child: Tells his friends that there are no "girl colors."

The first child: Was shielded from sugar and white flour until kindergarten. Other kids taunted him when he insisted that the rice cakes in his lunch box were cookies.

The second child: Ingested no sweets until her older brother went to kindergarten.

The third child: Teethed on siblings' Popsicle sticks. Sister mixed strawberry Quik into his bottle hoping that pink milk would turn him into a girl.

The first child: Played with new Lego sets. When he was obsessed with pirates, we bought pirates.

The second child: Pretended little Lego pirates were Barbie's babies.

The third child: Ingested Legos and Barbie shoes that he found on the floor and under the couch cushions.

The first child: Goes to piano lessons, soccer practice, French class and Tao Kwon Do.

The second child: Takes ballet.

The third child: Spends afternoons in the backseat driving to other kids' lessons.

The first child: Wants a puppy. Gets one.

The second child: Wants a kitten. Gets a little brother.

The third child: Wants a little brother. Gets sea monkeys.

The first child: Carries lunch (whole wheat bread, lean turkey, fruit) to school in a new lunch box.

The second child: Brings peanut butter in lunch box with brother's name on it.

The third child: Buys lunch.

The first child: Parents are convinced that he's a genius.

The second child: Parents think that she's gifted.

The third child: Parents are glad he has a sense of humor.

The first child: Birthday party features a three-layer cake made from scratch and decorated in appropriate theme.

The second child: Birthday party features a cake from the local bakery.

The third child: When's that kid's birthday?

Actually, that kid's birthday is coming up. He wanted to have a few friends sleep over to celebrate, but I have a better idea. This year, instead of a birthday party, I think someone should throw me a baby shower—the shower that I never had—the shower that I am owed. After all, my baby needs a lot of things. He's outgrown his sister's sneakers and his brother's old jeans are all ripped at the knees. His sea monkeys are dead and he's starting to suspect that pink just might be a girl color. The baby shower doesn't have to be elaborate, just a few finger sandwiches, a three-layer cake and plenty of brand-name clothes for a size eight-slim boy and—I'll be sure to take lots of pictures.

TOOTH-FAIRY TALES

I thought the jig was up.

My daughter, Perry, lost a tooth—not her first tooth, not a front tooth, just an ordinary, bottom row, baby tooth. Before I went to bed that night, I found an appropriately ethereal pink pad and a purple glitter pen in Perry's room and dashed off the obligatory note from the Tooth Fairy. I slid it under her pillow along with a shiny, gold Sacagawea dollar. The golden dollar required a special trip to the bank. My advice is: Don't bother. Your kids will think it's a big quarter.

The next morning, the household was awakened by an announcement from Perry's room that the Tooth Fairy had, indeed, landed. "Hey! Rip-off! She only left me a quarter!"

By the time she came to the breakfast table, my daughter had forgotten the money and turned her attention and her uncanny eye for detail to the Tooth Fairy's note.

"The Tooth Fairy's handwriting looks a lot like yours, Mom," she probed.

"Really? That's interesting," I feigned surprise.

"No, Mom, really. The way she makes her R's looks exactly the same as yours when you sign my report card."

I began to feel defensive. "They don't look the same to me," I said. "See, her "i's" are all dotted with little teeth and her handwriting is way fancier than mine." I tried to keep the panic out of my voice. "Besides," I added triumphantly, "I never sign your report cards with a purple glitter pen."

"Mom," she countered, "I have a pen that writes just like that. You probably stole it from my room." It was obvious that she was on to me. She knew the truth. "Mom," she glared at me with steely determination, "you are the Tooth Fairy!"

I was cornered. There was no way out. My mind raced as I tried to think of some way to save her innocence, to preserve her imagination and retain the last vestiges of her precious childhood. If you believe in fairies, clap your hands!

"You're right," I finally agreed. "I am the Tooth Fairy." She looked skeptical. "I never told you because I thought that it wouldn't be fair if the other kids in the neighborhood knew. They'd be jealous."

"Mom, come on," she pleaded. "Tell me the truth." I knew I had her.

"I am telling the truth," I explained. "The women in our family have been the Tooth Fairy for many generations. Do you think it's a coincidence that Grandma Helen is a dental hygienist?" That was the clincher. She was a believer.

"But how come I never see you going out at night to collect teeth and give kids money?"

"Sweetie," I explained with fairy-like patience, "you know how I'm always dashing off to all those PTO meetings?"

"Tooth-Fairy business?" she asked solemnly.

"Yep. And you're next in line. Just like *The Princess Diaries.*"

"Wow," she said. "I guess that's kind of cool."

She seemed a little shook up, a little overwhelmed by having so much to think about before breakfast. She was strangely silent. Perhaps she was mulling over her destiny, or maybe she was mentally poking holes in my story. Then, she pocketed the gold dollar and smiled. Genealogy is powerful stuff. Wait until Christmas when she figures out that her dad is Santa.

INDEPENDENCE DAY

The way I see it, my job as a parent is to put myself out of business. When my kids choose oatmeal over Coco Puffs, brush their teeth before bed without me losing my cool and remember where they left their soccer cleats, then I will congratulate myself on a job well done and book a cruise to Bora-Bora.

So far my job security seems assured. My kids have discovered that it's easier, faster and a lot more fun to yell "Maaaahhhhmm," than it is to unwrap a new roll of toilet paper, cut their own sandwiches or to get up and look under the couch for the television remote.

"Maaaahhhhmm!" my daughter screams from her bedroom. I gallop up the stairs, expecting bloodshed or at least a stubbed toe, but she hands me a wrinkled shirt and says, "Can you iron this for me?" I remind her, as I shoot steam onto her favorite, forty-dollar t-shirt from Abercrombie & Fitch, that in some countries girls her age are already married and ironing their own shirts as well as the shirts of their nine-year-old husbands.

"You do it better than me," she says with an endearing smile.

Maybe, but there are so many other things that she does so well. She can blow-dry her hair until it lies stick straight and re-program the car radio so that I can't find the oldies station. She can do her homework while she listens to her IPod, talks to eight friends on-line, paints her fingernails blue and eats popcorn. If only her skills were of a more practical nature, I might already be packing for Bora-Bora.

Lewis emerges wet from the tub and yells down the stairs. "Maaaahhhhmm! I need more toys in the tub," he demands.

"You can get them," I say in my most supportive voice.

"No, I can't. I'm all wet."

"Yes, you can," I assure him.

"No I can't."

Naked and dripping in the hallway, he has all the time in the world to debate while water puddles around his feet. I've discovered that my kids always have more time and infinitely more patience than me. So it's me who ends up mopping the hallway and fetching plastic WWF figures and a rubber-band-powered submarine as I mentally postpone the trip to Bora-Bora.

My oldest son is self-sufficient in so many ways. He can cook and consume a pound of bacon, download music from the Internet, and remove the batteries from our only working smoke alarm and insert them into his IPod speakers—all by himself. Yet, he cannot get on his bike and ride across town to a friend's house if it's cloudy, more than seventy two degrees or if the wind is blowing from the east. "Mom, can you drive me.... please?"

My kids still rely on me to wake them up every morning, to dole out lunch money, to do their laundry, to remind them to clean their rooms, to monitor their television viewing, to curtail their computer use, to referee fights, to determine punishments and to drive them all over town. Sure, that's what parents are for, but I think my kids need to start doing more for themselves and more for me. Over two centuries ago, it was a revolution that paved the way to independence for our country. Maybe that's what's needed at my house—revolution, or a one-way ticket to Bora Bora.

MOM INTERRUPTED

Remember the movie *Girl Interrupted*? I've often thought that if there was a movie made of my life, it would be called *Mom Interrupted* and though it wouldn't be set in a mental institution, it would take place at my house—which is pretty much the same thing.

Since I've become a parent, I haven't slept through the night, gone to the bathroom or talked on the phone without some kid interrupting me. There's something about a mom who is otherwise engaged that is especially tantalizing to a child—especially a mom on the phone.

A mom on the phone presents a particularly vulnerable target for any child who is suddenly weak with hunger, has been wounded by a sibling or is just plain bored. Kids also know that a mom on the phone is more apt to say "yes" to just about anything, just so that she can finish her conversation in relative peace.

My kids like to wait until I'm on a teleconference with my boss or negotiating with the credit card company before they ask if they can eat all of their Halloween candy, put a tube of toothpaste in the microwave or order an R-rated movie on pay-per-view. They know that when I am on the phone not only are my hands tied, but my response to any request will be tempered by the fact that whomever is on the line will hear what's going down.

While I'm on the phone with my son's teacher, my daughter wants to negotiate the terms of a sleepover. When I'm ordering take-out Chinese, my son slips his mediocre report card under my nose for a signature. If doesn't matter if the calls are outgoing or incoming, they will be interrupted. As soon as I pick up the receiver, I become hugely popular and am in demand to referee a fight, plunge the overflowing toilet and mop up cat hurl.

I have asked … even implored my children not to interrupt me while I am on the phone. "Unless there is a life-threatening situation," I say. "Unless there is blood." For a few days after my tirade they will comply and silently circle around my telephone conversations like sharks holding notes and dramatically pantomiming their requests.

Sometimes, in a quest for a quiet phone conversation, I lock myself in the bathroom. There, the acoustics make the party on the other end think that they are on speaker phone. They aren't. My phone doesn't have any special features. There's no caller ID, no call waiting, no speed dial. The only special function on my telephone is *Mom Interrupted*. Perhaps you'd like this service, too. But you'll have to act quickly. *Mom Interrupted* is only available to select households and just for a limited time (until the kids leave for college). If you'd like a free demonstration, just give me a call.

2

Accept No Substitutes

A Household Word: **Puberty**

Despite appearances, middle school is not populated by little boys and twenty-five-year-old hookers. Girls just mature faster ... much faster.

DO THE MATH

Last night, my son Lewis asked me to help him with his math homework. He is in the sixth grade. So, naturally, I was stumped.

I was baffled last year when he was in fifth grade and had to multiply fractions. I was useless when he was in fourth grade and asked for help with long division and I was seriously challenged by a third-grade worksheet that involved circling pictures of bears. Frankly, I thought that after going to college, getting married and being fruitful and multiplying, my math days were over.

"Maybe you should ask Dad for help," I suggested.

I admit, I'm no whiz at middle school math, but that's because in my daily life I never need to calculate any circumference or find the lowest common denominator. But ask me to plot the most direct route to a remote suburban soccer field, to divide two chocolate cupcakes among three children or to estimate the time it will take for the windshield on my minivan to defrost on a Monday morning when the temperature is twenty-two degrees Fahrenheit, and I've got answers. That's because although I may be lousy at math, I excel at Arith-mom-tic.

The mathematics of motherhood is very different from what they teach in school, I explained to Lewis. It's a lot more conceptual, highly theoretical and really, really advanced. For instance, I've learned that four grape popsicles and one lime popsicle divided by five kids equals nothing but trouble; that instant oatmeal takes practically five whole minutes to prepare; and that three little girls on a play date almost always results in a negative number. I've discovered that things don't always add up.

Just yesterday, Child Number Three was lurking around the house, driving me crazy. It was too wet to play outside, too boring inside and too early to start on homework.

"Call a friend," I suggested.

"What's Will's number?" he asked.

"Six-four-eight-seven-four-oh-seven," I answered brightly. I may not know the tenth digit of pi, but I've memorized a lot of phone numbers.

A few minutes later, the doorbell rang and one bored boy plus another bored boy (take away two grape popsicles) added up to an afternoon of wrestling in the playroom and Whiffle ball in the rainy street. Applaud my genius, but it was simply basic Arith-mom-tic. $1 + 1 = 0$.

But I shouldn't feel smug. Sure, according to conventional math, my nearly twenty years of being a mom practically qualify me as a child management expert. Heck, I've raised three kids through colic, toilet training and preschool. I've even helped them make sense out of the irrational numbers of puberty. I've learned that one teenage girl + twenty, forty-dollar t-shirts from Abercrombie & Fitch often equals nothing to wear. However, using higher Math-mom-tics, we discover that although I have logged nearly two decades of parenting experience, my kids have a combined total of forty-five years of being kids.

The time that they have spent asking me for snacks, barging into the bathroom and interrupting my phone calls exceeds the years that I've devoted to perfecting my parenting skills by more than two to one. Even if you add my husband's experience (and according to Arith-mom-tic his years don't count nearly as much as mine) as a parental unit, we are still clearly outnumbered.

Go figure.

MOMS I LUV 2 HATE

As a mom, I find that there are plenty of opportunities to feel inadequate. Just ask my daughter and she'll tell you how woefully dorky I am. But it's other moms who really shake my confidence and make me wonder if my kids would be better off as wards of the state. Here is a field guide to some of the moms who make me question why I ever decided to reproduce.

Looks Good at the Bus Stop Mom

At 7:30am, she escorts her perfect children to the corner with perfectly brewed coffee steaming in her travel mug. Her kids have their musical instruments, their fossils for show and tell, their book reports in crisp covers and their lunches. *Looks Good at the Bus Stop Mom* has blow-dried her hair and glossed her lips. She's never late; she's never wearing her pajama bottoms under her parka and she can always find the top to her travel mug. I hate her.

Clean Car Mom

It could be a Volvo wagon, a minivan or a Prius, the make doesn't matter. What's astounding (and infuriating) is that her car is showroom clean—always. No muddy art projects on the floor, no loose Hannah Montana CDs stuck between the seats. Bum a ride to the preschool fair and you'll never have to sweep petrified French fries off the seat of her car. This is the mother of the child who, when you drive the carpool, blithely asks "Why is your car so messy?" If her car was ever buried in an avalanche, she'd starve. Often seen driving to Talbots with *Looks Good at the Bus Stop Mom*. Think snow.

It's Alive Mom

Tadpoles are hatching in a bucket in her garage. There's a monarch cocoon in a jar in the kitchen that, under her care, will most certainly become a butterfly. I can't even keep a Chia pet, alive, but *It's Alive Mom* has two dogs, three guinea pigs and four rabbits that are litter-box trained. And guess what? Her cat is going to have kittens (Pleeeeassseeee? Can we have one?)! Every time your child returns from a play date at her house he is further convinced that you are really boring. And mean, too. "Why can't we have a kitten?"

Doesn't Buy White Bread Mom

Her kid comes to your house and lectures you on the shortcomings of white flour and the dangers of high fructose corn syrup. You introduce him to Pop Tarts and hope that his mom doesn't ask for details about the play date snacks. When your child returns from her house, he brings home a bear fashioned from whole wheat bread dough. "Tuesday is baking day at our house," *Doesn't Buy White Bread Mom* explains. Tuesday is pizza delivery day at our house. Wednesday is, too. Grrrr.

Martha Stewart Mom

No Chuck E. Cheese for this gal. She'd rather dress up like Glinda the Good and give each little guest a handcrafted pair of ruby slippers. The multi-tiered cake is an exact replica of the Emerald City (See *Teacher's Pet Mom*) and her cooperative husband, dressed as the Scarecrow, leads the scavenger hunt down the Yellow Brick Road that they've constructed in the backyard. I'm jealous of her sewing skills and her marriage. Pulling off a party like this would give me a nervous breakdown and my husband would never wear a scarecrow suit. Ever. For *Martha Stewart Mom*, it's a piece of cake. I think I hate her.

Teacher's Pet Mom

This woman spends more time with my kids than I do. She's always in the classroom being indispensible, introducing craft projects, passing our cupcakes (see *Martha Stewart Mom*) and reading out loud. She's the one who tells me that my son throws away most of the lunch I pack every day, that he rubs glue on his hands during art and that he still can't tie his shoes. Thanks, *Teacher's Pet Mom*!

College Prep Mom

She turns every moment into a learning experience. At snack time, she counts Cheerios with her toddler and categorizes the animal crackers by their genus. Her preschooler can read the ingredients on her organic juice boxes (see *Doesn't Buy White Bread Mom*) and the headlines in *Brain Child* magazine. Her dining room table is covered with projects that involve popsicle sticks and cold fusion. She enrolls her kids in summer camps that offer enriching indoor activities like "Phantasy Physics" or "Animatronics." Often seen at the Science Museum with *It's Alive Mom*.

So fellow moms, if you recognize yourself on this list, do me a favor. Keep being a part of my kids' lives so that they can taste homemade bread, attend magical birthday parties, watch tadpoles hatch and not trip over their shoelaces. Oh, and *Bus Stop Mom* ... try to look lousy once in a while.

A Parent's Guide to Middle School

Middle school can be a scary place. Not for eleven-year-olds who are itching to leave the warm and fuzzy confines of elementary school to eat lunch with kids who shave, but for parents who have to accept that their child is growing up and entering a world where lockers have combinations and where hormones lurk around every corner.

Fortunately, the middle-school curriculum is carefully structured, and the staff professionally trained to help children bridge the awkward period between the elementary years and high school. For most *parents*, however, the middle school experience is not a bridge, but a dark and mysterious tunnel that morphs our sweet babies into surly adolescents and makes us wonder, "Is it cocktail hour yet?"

As the mother of a recent eighth-grade graduate, I've learned a few things that I hope will shed some light into that developmental tunnel and make the next few years a little less terrifying:

1. **The weight of your child's backpack has no relationship to the amount of homework he has been assigned.** An eighty-pound child who drags home forty pounds of books and papers will still claim to have no homework.

2. **Kids who say that they have no homework should be required to clean their rooms and organize their backpacks.** Faced with this alternative, middle school students will often display remarkable powers of recall and suddenly remember that they have a science project due tomorrow.

3. **Never, ever pull up to the front steps of the school when you are driving your child to or picking her up from middle school.** No matter how heavy the backpack is, your child would rather walk an additional half block than risk having anyone discover that she has parents—especially parents as weird as you.

4. **Despite all appearances, middle school is not populated by little boys and twenty-five-year-old hookers.** Girls just mature faster ... much faster.

5. **Shut up and drive.** When the backseat is full of seventh-grade girls going to soccer practice or to the mall, the chauffeur gets the inside

scoop. Do not try to inject yourself into their conversation or sing along with Avril Lavigne. Just keep your eyes on the road, your hands on the wheel and your ears on the backseat.

6. **Know that even the most academically gifted middle school girl cares most about just three things: what she looks like, what her friends look like, and what her friends think she looks like.** In three years, the situation in the Middle East will still be a mess. Your kid can catch up on global events when she doesn't have to worry about pimples.

7. **If you want your middle-schooler to eat breakfast and get to school on time, assure her that her hair looks great.** Really. It's fabulous. It will get greasy if you touch it anymore. Now, eat some cereal and get out of here.

8. **Don't worry if your child says she's "popular."** Although the term "popular" can be a euphemism meaning that your daughter dates the high school track team, a child who boasts that she is "popular" is generally just … popular.

9. **Attend your child's athletic events, but do not speak to other parents or cheer audibly.** Never offer encouragement to your player by calling out "Run like a big boy!" or "That's Mommy's precious goalie."

10. **When middle school boys and girls talk about their peers "going out," this does not mean that they go to the movies, hold hands or even speak to each other.** These pairings are created by girls through a series of elaborately folded notes, text messaging and third-party conversations. Relaying these messages and folding the notes takes away time from other activities like homework and room cleaning. Parents should encourage platonic friendships and learn how to refold the notes.

11. **Four eighth-grade boys + twelve Dr. Peppers = one trashed TV room.**

12. **Discourage parties.** See #11. Forbid boy-girl parties unless this sounds like your idea of a swell Saturday: Your daughter runs upstairs in tears and locks herself in her bedroom, other girls leave in a huff and the boys stay until the chips run out. Analysis of the evening's events online and over the telephone detracts from homework and room cleaning for the rest of the school year.

13. **When you attend parent-teacher conferences and your daughter's math teacher says that she's a joy to have in class, don't look shocked and ask if you're in the right room.** Simply smile and say, "Thank you."

SLOW CHILDREN

"Slow as molasses in January." That's what my grandmother would say. But today, with the advent of central heating, global warming, and slice 'n bake cookies, molasses flows fast, nobody bakes and those folksy expressions don't have much relevance—not in my life, anyhow.

In my house, the expression has been revised to "slow as Lewis in February." My youngest son has no sense of urgency and nothing I do can make him hustle. When I rouse him for school, the first thing he says is: "Hold on, five more minutes." Then he burrows deeper under the covers.

Getting him up for school requires constant prodding and I find myself shrieking out the time like a banshee Big Ben: "It's six-forty-five! Get up! It's seven-ten! Go brush your teeth! It's seven-fifteen! Do you have your backpack? It's seven-thirty! Hurry up!" I'm telling you, the kid is slow.

It's probably my fault. After all, he was born nearly two weeks after his due date. That should have been a warning. I should have done something, like downed castor oil or gone bungee jumping. Instead, I waddled into my tenth month and wept when the neighbors asked, "Aren't you ever going to have that baby?"

I should have been induced. Maybe that would have given my son a respect for deadlines and reinforced the concept of punctuality. Instead, I listened to my midwife, who advocated a hands-off approach and suggested that I monitor the fetal kicks, take non-stress tests and let nature take its course. That course took nine months and eighteen days. I'm sure that when my son was called out of the womb and into the world, he told Mother Nature, "Hold on. I'm coming ... just five more minutes."

Like my grandmother's molasses, the agonizing slowness of my youngest child is especially pronounced in the wintertime. Maybe it's the addition of mittens, scarves and boots that makes simply getting out of the house an ordeal. Just this morning, I waited while he found his mittens and put them on, then took them off so that he could tie his shoes, then put them back on again, took them off to zip his jacket and put them on again. It was interminable.

"Hurry up," I urged.

We walked to the school bus stop. A few snowflakes swirled in the breeze. My glasses fogged up and my coat looked like an ad for dandruff shampoo. I carried Lewis' backpack and his saxophone so that he could scamper to the bus stop unencumbered. Still, he lagged behind.

"Hurry up!" I yelled and picked up the pace. I looked back to see if he was hurrying. He wasn't. He was standing on the sidewalk, immobile, looking at the sleeve of his navy blue parka. I felt my frustration building. If he missed the bus, I'd have to drive him and then I'd be late.

"Mom! Come here, hurry!" he said, motioning to me with a mittened hand.

I trudged back. "Lew, we're going to be late," I growled.

"Look," he said, holding out his arm.

Against the dark blue nylon of his jacket were perfect snowflakes. Each one was like a tiny work of art—each different and each beautiful. Each snowflake floated onto the jacket at its own pace and then melted away. I was glad Lewis noticed them and I wondered … could the snowflakes teach us a lesson on this hectic morning?

Nah. Hurry up!

THIS IS ONLY A TEST

The Standardized Achievement Test, or SAT, is used by colleges around the country to determine if a child has the fajitas to excel at a particular university. The more competitive the school, the higher the median SAT score of the incoming freshman class. Parents take these tests extremely seriously. We somehow feel that our kids' test scores are a reflection not only of our children's intelligence (which of course they inherit from us) but also of our parenting ability. I know I do. My oldest son just took the SAT's and received his scores on-line. Let's just say Harvard won't be knocking on his door and it's all my fault.

Maybe if I hadn't let him go to the late show of the *Matrix Reloaded* at our local theater the night before the test, he might have been more focused. Maybe if I had made him scrambled eggs and bacon instead of letting him eat a bowl of Cap'n Crunch for breakfast, he would have felt more alert. Maybe we should have hired a tutor or signed him up for one of those test prep classes. Or maybe I should have begun grooming him for the SATs before he even entered high school.

I knew I should have bought a *Stim-Mobile*. Those popular black and white crib mobiles were just gaining popularity when I was pregnant with Nathan. They are supposed to help babies focus and recognize patterns. Instead, when my son was born, I hung fuzzy, pastel bunnies over his crib. Who knows? If I had purchased a *Stim-Mobile* he might have eked out a few more points on the spatial reasoning section of the Math SAT. If only college admission offices would take a look at my son's Apgar scores. Those were perfect.

"The registration deadline for the October test is next week," I gently remind my son. "You could retake it and up your scores. We could hire a tutor."

"Chill out, Mom!" he advises as he fiddles with an amplifier in his room. "My scores are fine. I don't need to take the test again."

Indeed, he has already taken the test twice. The second time, after an intense weekend test-prep class, his math score dropped a full thirty points. Who knows how far they might plummet on a third try?

I blame myself.

Maybe I should have played Mozart instead of Meatloaf on the way home from the hospital, bought him flash cards instead of baseball cards and gotten him *Hooked on Phonics*. Now it's too late to turn him into a prodigy.

If I had only been more diligent about taking my prenatal vitamins! But who could predict that scientists would find a correlation between folic acid and IQ?

I hate chicken livers and turnip greens, but I would have gladly choked them down by the platter if had know they would help get my kid into the Ivy League.

"Are you sure you won't take the test again?" I pushed just one more time.

"Mom," my son said, looking at me firmly. "You are taking this SAT thing way too seriously. I did fine. It's just a test. It's only a number. My SAT score is not the only reflection of who I am."

Turns out, he's a pretty smart kid. And, despite his mother's neurosis, come September some lucky college will probably count him among their freshman class. Still, I think it couldn't hurt to hang a *Stim-Mobile* over the bed in dorm room ... even if it's not at Harvard.

GOING HAI-CUCKOO

Aside from composing excuse notes to my kids' teachers, I don't do much that's really creative. I've told myself that I'm too busy to compose poetry or pen a best seller. I have stuff to do—stuff like change the litter box and look for my car keys. I don't have a lot of time to decoupage cigar boxes, or take up scrapbooking or write in iambic pentameter. Then I discovered haiku.

> *Please excuse my child,*
> *His absence was all my fault,*
> *He had no clean clothes.*

A mom must have invented these quick little poems. Now, I'm addicted. I find myself actually thinking in beats of five-seven-five and finding a haiku in almost every situation.

> *Children rush inside,*
> *Boots are off and puddles form*
> *On my kitchen floor.*

My children, I find, are a constant source of inspiration.

> *A cruel winter trick,*
> *February vacation*
> *And three kids with strep.*

I like to write at night when the house is quiet

> *The kids are asleep.*
> *The dirty dishes can wait*
> *But the wine cannot.*

Sometimes, I just try to capture the beauty of the season ...

One winter blessing,
The ten pounds I just can't lose
Hides under goose down.

Snow falls from the sky.
I turn on the radio.
Please, don't list my town.

In February,
The Christmas toys are silent.
The batteries, dead.

Or compose a tribute to my Valentine ...

Husband is that you?
Or a fierce tiger that roars
On the couch, asleep.

Or to males in general ...

Super Bowl Sunday,
Men come to my house with beer.
I flee to the mall.

I'm sure that February vacation week will provide ideal conditions for poetic thought ...

Teacher, are you glad
To be child-free for a week?
Or are you a mom?

The beauty of the ancient art of haiku is that it suits a modern mom's lifestyle perfectly. While you're on hold with the credit-card company or driving the carpool, you can put those spare moments to good use by creating poetry. If February vacation week doesn't provide enough inspiration, pour yourself some sake.

3

Almost Housebroken

A Household Word: **Flushable**

Do not buy a ferret. Even if your child throws himself on the floor of Petco and sobs as he imagines the inconsolable sorrow of continuing to live without a foot-long, furry companion. They smell. Check out the ads for used ferrets on Craig's List. There is a reason that you can get two ferrets, a three-story cage and a twenty-pound bag of ferret-chow for free.

THE LIVING DEAD

This past summer, we visited one of those touristy shops at the beach and I broke down and bought my son a hermit crab. For Lewis, part of the appeal was that the crab's shell was painted with the logo of the Boston Red Sox, his favorite baseball team. For me, the hermit crab seemed like a good alternative to more complex life forms like geckos, guinea pigs and iguanas.

"His name is Bruce," my son said lovingly as the crab clamped onto his finger and drew blood. "I think he likes me!" On the ride home, Lewis sat in the backseat with a cardboard container on his lap and cooed to Bruce through the air holes.

"Why are you talking to that crab, you moron," Lewis' teenage sister said. "Crabs can't hear you, and even if they could they don't even have brains. They're like lobsters. I think we should cook him."

"Don't listen to her, Brucey," my son hissed into the box. "She's just jealous."

At home we found an old ten-gallon aquarium, one that is haunted by the ghosts of deceased goldfish and long-dead gerbils, and transferred Bruce to his permanent digs.

"Bruce needs a more interesting habitat," my son said as he proceeded to arrange Lego guys and plastic dinosaurs in the tank. The crab seemed unimpressed. At the store, he had been seemed lively, but here, amid a T-Rex and sword-wielding pirates, he seemed a little lethargic.

"Maybe he's just tired from the long drive," I suggested.

We went to our local pet shop to stock up on hermit crab food—even though I suspected that Bruce wouldn't live to consume much of the fishy powder that Lewis piled into his tiny seashell dish. We also bought a sea sponge, so Bruce wouldn't become dehydrated, a bag of neon orange pebbles, to mimic his natural habitat, and we blew seventeen dollars on a plaster castle that might have added a little more quality to the short life of the now-dead goldfish. This was one lucky crab.

"Bruce is going to be *soooo* happy," my son beamed as he festooned the tank with our new purchases. He also added a Spider-Man action figure, a handful of marbles and several Hot Wheels cars. The environment in the tank was so rich, so stimulating, that it was hard to even locate the crab. When I did, he looked suspiciously ... dead.

"I think that you might want to take a look at Bruce," I said in a gentle tone.

"Whadayya mean?" Lewis asked.

"Well, he's not really moving," I said.

"That's because he's sleeping," my son quipped.

Who was I to question his expertise? Maybe he *was* just sleeping. So I took a pair of tongs from the kitchen and moved Bruce into a realistic pose near the sponge. Maybe some water would perk him up.

"See, Mom, I told you he was just asleep," my son said at bedtime as he diligently dumped more food into the seashell dish. "Bruce is drinking water now."

"Did you see him walk there?" I asked.

"No, but he's drinking; he's fine," my son assured me.

The next morning, the crab's thirst was apparently still not quenched. While Lewis brushed his teeth, I used the tongs to reposition Bruce at the door of the castle. He looked good there. In fact, he stayed in that position for several days—until Lewis needed to retrieve the Spider-Man figure.

"Hey! Bruce is guarding the castle!" Lewis exclaimed when he noticed the crab's new post. I pondered Bruce's next move and wondered how long I should carry on the charade.

I've thought about replacing Bruce with a live crab, but our pet store only sells fish. Even if I could locate a suitable double, I'm not sure that I could lure a new crustacean into Bruce's Red Sox shell or that I could successfully evict the current (albeit deceased) occupant.

Turns out, a dead hermit crab is a pretty good pet. He doesn't eat anything, his cage never needs cleaning and the faint stench of rotting shellfish emitting from Lewis' room not only adds a waterfront ambience to the whole house, it has given our geriatric cat a renewed sense of purpose. The only maintenance required, is periodically moving the shell to simulate lifelike activity. The dead crab's antics have kept my son amused now for over a month. Sometimes Bruce is atop the sponge "drinking." Other days he's positioned near his food dish, and sometimes he's wedged inside the Hot Wheels convertible, ready to race around the tank.

"I like Bruce," my son said yesterday. "But when he dies, I'm going to make a necklace out of his shell."

I can't think of a more fitting memorial.

Sit, Stay, Roll Your Eyes ... Good Boy!

We have a new addition at our house. Not a baby (thank goodness), but a puppy. If you think that I got the dog for my three kids, you're wrong. I got the dog for me.

With two teenagers in my house, I need to balance their criticism of my clothes, my jokes and my driving ability with someone who will give me unconditional approval and wet kisses. I want someone to roll over, not roll their eyes.

My friends without teenagers don't understand. "A puppy is just like a baby," they say. "Your kids are barely out of diapers. Why would you want to start the whole housebreaking process all over again?"

I have to admit, during the first few weeks of new puppy parenthood I've been sleep deprived and slightly frazzled, but in lots of ways having a puppy is better than having a baby. My nipples aren't sore from nursing, and I know that in fourteen years the dog won't be a surly adolescent; he'll probably be dead.

Having a dog is easier than having kids, too. I can leave the puppy locked up when I go out and the ASPCA thinks it's just fine. If I tried to crate my teenagers (and sometimes it seems like a pretty good idea) the child welfare authorities might not be real sympathetic.

When I come home (even if I've locked him in a crate), the dog is happy to see me. He's more than happy. He's ecstatic, and he covers me with those wet kisses. My teens don't even bother to look up from the computer screen. They just ask, "When's supper?"

When it's dinnertime, the dog thinks that I'm Julia Child. He is happy to lick up any crumb that falls on the kitchen floor. He never complains when I serve him dry puppy chow in the same bowl for two weeks in a row. In fact, he likes it.

My teenagers aren't impressed with my culinary skills. "Eww ... meatloaf," they complain. "Why can't we get pizza?" Maybe I should serve them puppy chow, too.

The dog always comes when I call. My teens can't hear me call them unless I jump in front of the television screen and yell. Even then, they don't move. They simply roll their eyes and say, "Hold on, I'm about to kill these trolls."

The dog never rolls his eyes. When I talk to him, his ears perk up and he looks at me intently and listens. He thinks I'm fascinating. My teenagers think that I am a hopeless geek.

The dog doesn't run up the phone bill with text messages about his love life or put perfectly clean clothes into the laundry hamper. He doesn't need braces or a ride to the mall.

The dog doesn't want clothes from Abercrombie and Fitch. In fact, Abercrombie doesn't even carry his size. The dog never asks me for money or borrows my good leather boots to walk to school when it's raining.

Unlike my kids, the dog actually plays with his toys and seems grateful for the one or two that I have brought home from Petco. The dog doesn't mind if I sing along with the car radio.

I can walk the dog around the block and he's not embarrassed to be seen with me. He doesn't get mad or even roll his eyes when people comment on how much we look alike. In fact, he looks flattered.

I'm pretty sure that the dog will never deplete my life savings by spending four years at an expensive, private college drinking beer. He probably won't even go to college (okay, maybe a state school). He is, however, enrolled in Canine Kindergarten. Tuition is only seventy dollars and they promise that in eight weeks he'll learn to walk on a leash, sit and stay.

I just hope he never learns to roll his eyes.

8AM CAT/DENT

Yesterday, I got a postcard in the mail. It was from my veterinarian reminding me that our cat needs to have her teeth cleaned. Yeah, I'll get right on that. Maybe after I put all the baby pictures into albums and take down the Christmas lights. I mean I can't even get myself to the dentist twice a year.

I love the cat, but tending to her dental hygiene is not at the top of my to-do list. Right now, my list is topped with driving my kids to soccer practice and Little League games and piano recitals and swimming lessons and fifth-grade play rehearsal. In between, we squeeze in checkups for summer camp, orthodontist appointments, shoe shopping, returning overdue videos, looking for missing library books, parent/teacher conferences, birthday parties, running to the drugstore at 11pm for emergency poster board and ... oh, yeah, school and work. Even Daylight Savings Time doesn't save enough time to get everything done. So the cat's teeth go unscraped.

From September to mid-May, we're busy. But in June, when everything comes to a thrilling, end-of-the-school-year crescendo, the schedule gets kicked up a notch and we go from being merely active to being actively out-of-control.

Having three kids has seriously compromised my mental faculties, so I need to write everything down. That means that in this age of handheld electronic devices, I am a slave to the big paper calendar that hangs on the kitchen wall. Every appointment, rehearsal and practice is represented by cryptic notes detailing who, what, where and when. "5P/Sphs" means that my daughter Perry has soccer practice at the high school at 5pm. "L/CWDRtights!" reminds me that Lewis has a dress rehearsal for the play *Charlotte's Web* and that he needs to wear tights. "PS/$5" means that the permission slip and money is due for the field trip to the fish hatchery ("My mom can drive!"). But it's the stuff that's not on the calendar that really puts me over the edge.

"Mom, I need a black skirt for the concert tonight!" my daughter wails at four o'clock in the afternoon.

"Mom, we're supposed to bring cupcakes for the cast party. Pink ones," my son says as we are headed to the final performance.

"Mom! Our team won the division so now we get to go to the Regionals!" my oldest son announces. "I told Coach you could drive."

While the kids are happily flitting from one enriching experience to the next, my role is mainly to drive and wait. I drive to the school and wait outside for chorus practice to end. I drive to the soccer field in the rain and wait for them to call the game. I drive my daughter to piano lessons, drop off my son at play rehearsal and promise that somehow I will pick them both up at four-thirty.

The kids change their clothes in the car as we rush from one activity to the next. Family dinners have been replaced with a bagel in the backseat and conversation is reduced to a barrage of questions as we race out the door:

"Do you have your cleats?"

"Are we picking up Jason?"

"Where's my script?"

"Do I have to wear tights?"

Yesterday, as I penciled in another reminder on the June calendar,"5thGRD" (fifth-grade graduation), I peeked ahead to July and breathed a sigh of relief. There, just a page away, are gloriously blank summer days. No soccer, no play rehearsals, no Little League, no chorus. Everything just ends. The page is empty except for a freshly penciled note near the end of the month that cryptically reads "8am/CatDent."

ONE MOM'S MEAT

Everyone agrees that turkey is a fundamental part of Thanksgiving. Even my Italian sister-in-law, who thinks the Pilgrims ate lasagna, concurs that turkey is, at the very least, an important side dish. It was with that sentiment in mind that I set out to procure a bird that would not only feed the fifteen adults and children coming to my house for the holiday meal, but also provide ample leftovers for those staying through the weekend.

An ordinary specimen wouldn't do. So when our local newspaper ran an article about a place that raised organic, free-range turkeys, I called and ordered a big one. It seemed like a delicious and politically correct alternative to the frozen, foolproof, self-basting birds from the supermarket. Plus, I figured a trip to the turkey farm would be a new family tradition—like chopping your own Christmas tree, only with poultry.

On the day our dinner was to be, errrr.... dressed, I rounded up the kids. "Who wants to drive out to the country and visit a turkey farm?" I asked.

"Can we stop at the mall?" my daughter asked.

"No, we're just going to get the Thanksgiving turkey."

"I'm thinking of becoming a vegetarian," she said. "Is Aunt Toni bringing lasagna?"

Visions of a Walton-esque afternoon were rapidly fading. The only taker was my youngest son, Lewis, and he was looking to bargain. "I'll go," he said, "but only if I don't have to eat turnips on Thanksgiving."

"Okay," I agreed hastily.

"And I get extra whipped cream on my pie and I don't have to give my bed to the cousins."

"It's a deal," I said and we got into the car.

With a fuzzy printout from MapQuest and vague directions from the newspaper article, we headed to the farm. We drove for an hour; past housing developments, bowling alleys and strip malls. "This doesn't look like the country," Lewis commented.

I reached for the crumpled map on the floor and squinted at it. "We still have a ways to go. Look for a big coffee stain up ahead."

"There's the farm!" Lew shouted. Sure enough, a crudely painted sign read "Turkies" and pointed up a narrow gravel road. As a person who is dependent on spell check, I should have seen this as an omen. Instead, I told myself that it was charming. "Now we're in the country," Lewis confirmed as the car lurched over rocks and the rusted mufflers and hubcaps of customers that had claimed turkeys before us. We drove through the dust, poised to brake for any free-range turkeys that might bound from the bushes. After several miles, the theme from *Deliverance* began to run through my head. The road dead-ended at a patch of dirt and a double-wide trailer. The banjo music in my brain was getting louder.

I guess I expected the farm to look like Old MacDonald's, with a gobble, gobble here, a kindly farmer there, and fluffy, free-range birds running up to greet us. Instead, a burly guy in a bloody apron appeared in the doorway.

"Stay here," I whispered to Lewis as I handed him the cell phone. "If I'm not back in five minutes, dial 911." I got out of the car.

"Your name Band?" the bloody behemoth bellowed. I nodded tentatively and followed him into the trailer. "Stay here," he snarled and ducked out a back door. I froze, listening for the sound of an ax but all I could hear was my son beeping the horn in the van. I motioned for him to come in and he scampered out of the car with the cell phone. We waited.

"Where are the turkeys?" Lew whispered.

"Beats me. It's probably better not to know."

Suddenly, the turkey terminator burst through the back door. He had a murderous gleam in his eye and Lewis says there were feathers in his beard. He handed me a package wrapped in plastic. It was as heavy as a load of wet laundry and it was still warm.

"Twenty minutes a pound at 325°," he growled as he stashed my check into a shoebox. It wasn't exactly the Butterball Turkey Hotline, but it was somewhat comforting.

Back in the car, Lewis and I laughed with relief.

"Poor Al," Lewis said as he patted the plastic bag on the back seat next to him.

"Who?" I asked peering into the rearview mirror.

"Our turkey," Lewis replied. "I named him Al. I think he's leaking."

I handed Lewis a wad of tissues from the glove compartment. "Don't get too attached," I warned.

At home, we entombed Al on the bottom shelf of the fridge, where he displaced a bag of bruised apples, two cartons of eggs and a head of dead lettuce. Now, I check on him every couple of hours to make sure that he hasn't sprung to life or sprung a leak. I'm sure that on Thanksgiving Day I'll be glad that we risked our lives to get an organic, free-range turkey and that Al will be delicious.

If not, there's always lasagna.

IF YOU GIVE MOUSE A CHEEZ-IT

"Moommmmmm!!!! Eeeeeeeeeekk!!!!" I raced downstairs and found my daughter, Perry, standing on the kitchen table. *"Mouse!"* she gasped as if that explained why she looked like she was dancing at Greek taverna.

Sure, my housekeeping standards are what some call "relaxed," and it's true that our obese cat rarely ventures from the couch, but I blame the recent rodent invasion on my kids.

"Take the dirty dishes out of your room," I yell as they gaily toss popcorn toward their heads while they do homework in the dining room. "Throw the pizza boxes into the trash!" I plead when they have friends over to play video games in the den. Those leftover crusts will attract rats," I predict. "We'll have vermin." And now we do. Okay, we don't have rats, but we have mice or, at least, a mouse.

"There's no such thing as just one mouse," my husband, Harris, warned ominously.

"We'll get a mousetrap," I assured my daughter. "We'll catch it."

"Trap?" Perry cried from her table-top perch." How can you be so cruel? It's a living creature. You can't just murder it."

Lewis, wandered into the kitchen, his arm deep into a box Cheez-Its. "Who's Mom gonna murder?"

"You, if you don't stop dropping food all over the house," I said. "We have a mouse."

"Cool! Can I have it for a pet?"

My husband and son headed out, in search of weapons of mouse destruction, and returned with a Havahart trap. The theory behind the Havahart is that you catch the mouse unharmed, then set it free at your neighbor's house, where it becomes their problem.

That night, I baited the Havahart with peanut butter and placed it behind the stove, ironically, out of the cat's reach. In the morning, we had a mouse.

"Let's call him Nibbles," Lewis said as I dumped our tiny captive into an empty aquarium. Frankly, I could think of more accurate verbs to describe creature now cowering in the corner of the fish tank producing copious amounts of droppings. The cat, intrigued by the concept of a pre-caught mouse got off the couch and pawed at the glass.

I'd like to say that Nibbles looked like a Disney character with big brown eyes and a little pink nose. But he didn't. He was black and kind of greasy looking—like he had been hanging out with a tough crowd behind the stove. He was fat, too, with a belly that testified to the bounty of Cheez-It crumbs in our house.

"Can I keep him in my room?" Lewis asked.

"No, I said envisioning bubonic plague, hantavirus and rabies. "Let's put him in the basement. "I lugged the aquarium with the quaking mouse downstairs and placed it on the washer.

Lewis ripped up a newspaper and stuffed it into the aquarium along with the cardboard tube from a brand new roll of paper towels. Then he added some Cheez-Its and an apple core. It was plush accommodations for a mouse who, had he been trapped by a more clear-thinking family, would be dead. But, tomorrow morning, while my kids were still asleep, I would simply walk down the street to my neighbor's house (the ones with the obnoxious leaf blower) and let Nibbles go. Problem solved.

"I just want to stay here and watch him for a while." Lewis leaned on the washer and stared dreamily at the mouse that was burrowing into the newspaper.

Now, it's unusual for anything, other than Halo3, to hold Lewis' attention for more than fifteen minutes. So I was surprised when I went downstairs an hour later and saw him still concentrating on the mouse.

"Mom, there's something wrong with Nibbles," Lew said. "I think he's gnawed off his leg. There's a bloody stump."

This is why I hate pets. I gingerly lifted the shredded newspaper to get a better look. "It's not a bloody stump," I reported to Lewis. Turns out, Nibbles belly wasn't obese from a diet of junk food crumbs. In fact, he wasn't overweight at all. He was pregnant. "It's a baby mouse. Nibbles is a mom."

"Sa … wheet!" Lew breathed. "Wait. Don't mice do eat their young?"

"They do if they're smart," I told him.

In a just a few hours, Nibbles had produced a pile of writhing, slug-shaped newborns. "Let's give Nibbles time to be alone with her babies," I said and, while Lew went on on-line to research the care of infant *mus musculus*, I put more peanut butter in the Havahart trap.

RIGHT FROM THE GECKO

Buying presents for preteens is tough. For my son's twelfth birthday, he said he wanted a dirt bike, a cell phone, an Xbox 360 or a gecko.

Hmmm ... let me think. The dirt bike was totally out of the question. An Xbox 360 costs $400 and would be another screen for me to monitor. A cell phone has monthly charges and text messaging fees and I'm sure Lewis would lose it within a week. Then there's the gecko, which he says would be educational, and only costs six dollars and ninety-nine cents. Frankly, it was a no-brainer. We got Lewis the Xbox. No seriously, we bought a gecko. But, now I am thinking that the Xbox might have been a better choice. Turns out, there are hidden costs that come with a seven dollar pet.

We already owned a ten-gallon aquarium, which had formerly housed a hermit crab. So, I scrubbed it clean and we went to the pet superstore to pick out a gecko. Turns out, a baby leopard gecko needs more than just a clean tank.

According to the teenage reptile expert at the store, geckos are desert creatures and for their health and well-being, you must recreate the climate of sub-Saharan Africa in their habitat. That means that in addition to the gecko, the tank would also contain a heating pad to maintain an eighty-five degree temperature ($29.99), a ceramic basking lamp with realistic moon light simulator ($24.99) and a $16 light bulb that gets hot enough to make toast. The gecko also required a synthetic rock to climb ($12.99) and a piece of sterilized bark ($4.99) to rub against when it sheds its skin (had I known about the skin shedding, I might have gone with the cell phone). Lewis also insisted on two plastic plants ($5.00) for added feng shui.

"What about food?" I asked the lizard wizard.

"They eat crickets," he said.

"Live crickets?"

"Yep."

"Ewwww," I thought.

"Cool," said Lewis.

Conveniently, the pet store sells crickets. It's kind of like buying pets for your pet. The crickets come in plastic bags, but the gecko guy said that our crickets couldn't live in the bag for more than a few hours. They would suffocate or chew through the plastic and escape. My priority was that our crickets remained captive. So I purchased a Cricket Corral ($7.99), where they would be under maximum security, but could still live, fall in love and possibly reproduce before being consumed by the gecko. I bought a container of cricket food ($3.99) and a little sponge ($1.25) so they could enjoy a tiny drink with their last meals.

I also bought vitamin powder that the sales clerk said we should sprinkle on the crickets before they are introduced to the gecko.

"It's simple," he said. "Just put the crickets in a baggie, add a teaspoon of powder and toss gently."

"Just like Shake 'n Bake," I thought.

According to the gecko guy, our little lizard would consume five to ten crickets every day.

"Until it matures," he said. "Then you can also feed it pinkies." I stared blankly. "Newborn mice," he explained.

"Ewww," I thought.

"Cool," said Lewis.

"Let's stick with crickets for now," I said, as the sales clerk handed Lewis a bag of fifty scuttling crickets that cost twenty-two cents each.

Then I did the math. Eight crickets times twenty-two cents. That's $1.76 every day. That's $12.32 a week, $640.64 a year! I didn't tell my son, but that is way more than an Xbox 360.

"Ah ... how long do these geckos usually live?" I asked, trying to sound casual.

"With proper care, about twenty years," said the gecko guy with a sadistic little smile.

Turns out, Lewis was right. Owning a gecko is educational. I've already learned that a $6.99 gecko may sound like a good deal, but it's way more than I bargained for.

4

What's That Green Stuff?

A Household Word: **Grown-up**

Go play outside. Finish your dinner. Take a bath. Go to bed. If this sounds like a perfect day, you're not a kid.

HIDE AND SNEAK*

My kids don't trust me. It's not because I snoop in their rooms, or listen in on their phone conversations or rummage through their backpacks without permission. It's because I mess with their food. That's right. I plead guilty to sneaking healthy stuff into their abysmal, beige diets. As the mother of three picky eaters, it's my duty.

Left to their own devices, my kids would eat only pasta (with butter, no sauce) pancakes and pizza. Oh, they also like Pez. You'll notice that all of these foods have something in common. They all contain: NO VEGETABLES!

Yet, somehow my kids have survived—even seemingly thrived—without green beans, broccoli, peppers, lettuce, kale, Swiss chard, Brussels sprouts, eggplant, squash, spinach or asparagus. But I've read the USDA recommendations. They say that kids should consume two and a half cups of vegetables every day. Are they kidding? My children haven't eaten that many vegetables in their lifetimes—unless you count candy corn. Yet, when I asked my pediatrician about the long-term ramifications of an all-carb diet, he didn't seem overly concerned. He said that if they eat ice cream and peanut butter and pop an occasional multivitamin, they'll probably be fine.

Still, I worry that they'll contract scurvy, or become constipated or get cavities. I imagine them growing up without ever tasting a fresh-picked tomato, my mother's candied sweet potatoes or the Cobb Salad at Chili's. So I keep pushing the vegetables.

Now I didn't just fall off the turnip truck. I know that there are tricks that parents use to get their kids to eat vegetables. And I know that they don't work, because I've tried them all. I've cut carrots into coins and staged treasure hunts. I've played "hungry dinosaur" with broccoli trees. I've poured cheese sauce onto cauliflower, dipped green peppers into ranch dressing and smeared peanut butter over everything else. I've carved radish roses, created clown faces with snow peas and used a quart of canola oil to make sweet potato fries. I've even enlisted my kids to help shop for, cook and grow their own vegetables. Nothing works. At dinner time, they still approach anything from the plant kingdom like contestants on Fear Factor facing a plate of Madagascar cockroaches.

So, I've had to get a little sneaky. I'm not proud of the deception, but, I have only my children's health at heart. I started small. First, I added a dollop of canned pumpkin to the pancake mix, and they ate it up. Then, I sprinkled a teaspoon of chopped spinach into the pizza sauce. They didn't suspect a thing. So I got a little bolder. I grated zucchini into the pancake batter and tossed in some flax seed. I threw a handful of broccoli florets into the pizza sauce and mixed the mozzarella cheese with tofu. This time they noticed.

"There's green stuff in my pancakes!?" my son said, recoiling with horror. "It's mold!"

"It's just a little zucchini," I said in my most produce-loving voice. "Try it, it's delicious."

"Ewwwwww ... no way. I hate zucchini! Yuck."

They were on to me. Now, they approach every meal with suspicion. They examine their dinners like they are food tasters for the Czar.

"What's in this pizza?" my daughter says, sniffing her slice. "It smells funny."

"Can I see the box that the macaroni came in?"

"Is this the same bread you usually buy?"

It's not easy. In fact, I've had to discover new tricks. But it's all for their own good. Did you know that lima beans can fit into a Pez dispenser? Trust me.

Note: I wrote this when Jessica Seinfeld was still using an E-Z Bake Oven.

A WING AND A PRAYER

As I was planning my Thanksgiving dinner menu, it suddenly hit me. My kids won't eat any of this stuff. The sweet potatoes, the turnips, the cranberry relish—even the turkey doesn't coordinate with their culinary color palette, which consists primarily of white, blue and neon orange. If my kids could design their own Thanksgiving feast, it would be Froot Loops.

Maybe it's my fault. Maybe if I had exposed them to more exotic foods when they were babies, they would eat more than macaroni and cheese. Maybe if I had nibbled on chevre and mango chutney while I nursed my newborns, they would be willing to try food that doesn't come in a box (cereal, Jell-O, Kraft dinner, pizza and McDonald's Happy Meals).

Other parents (the ones whose kids snarf down foods like hummus and broccoli rabe) have loads of advice. "Just let them try new foods," they urge me. Yeah, right. Just help me pry their little mouths open while I force a little leafy something between their clenched jaws. Is a bite of kale worth years of therapy? I don't think so. Force-feeding is not part of my family dinner fantasy.

I thought we'd be the Walton's. I imagined that when I became a mom, my apple-cheeked children would beam thankfully at me as I heaped their plates with nutritious home-cooked meals. In reality, I put out cold cereal and peanut butter when my gang of three pronounces the dinner entrée to be "sickening." Can they really thrive on white bread, Cheerios and strawberries? My pediatrician seems to think so. When I asked him about my picky eaters, he said "Do they eat ice cream? Of course, I said. "Do they eat peanut butter?" "With Fluff," I replied. "Then they're fine," he assured me. "Don't worry."

But I do worry. It's not that I'm so concerned about their health; I'm more worried that they will grow up with no memories of home cooking. My warmest childhood recollections are of my Hungarian grandmother serving up steaming plates of chicken paprikas, my mother hand rolling hundreds of Swedish meatballs. My kids' only mealtime memories will be of me boiling water and ripping open packets of orange, cheese-flavored powder.

Child-development experts say that youngsters' discerning palettes are a survival mechanism that keeps them from eating stuff like poisonous mushrooms, broken glass and used condoms. And while the menu at our house won't kill them—if my kids if they don't expand their mealtime repertoire—I just might. This year, I've even made some changes to our traditional Thanksgiving menu that I hope will entice my kids to make their Thanksgiving feast more than just a roll with butter.

Gone are the mashed turnips and the creamed onions. Welcome corn on the cob and macaroni and cheese casserole. Gone is the century-old family recipe for mincemeat pie. Instead, I'll be serving chocolate pudding pie (a good source of calcium) with graham cracker crust. This year, if my kids promise to try a little bit of everything on the table, I promise that when they are all grown up and I come to their house for Thanksgiving, I'll eat Froot Loops.

INDIVIDUAL TASTE

I have three kids and I've done my best to raise them to be independent, free-thinking individuals. I've encouraged them to buck the crowd, to just say no and to not jump off of bridges, even when everyone else is diving headfirst into shallow water. I figured that by rearing three rugged individualists, they would be less likely to be bullied on the playground, pressured into sniffing glue or convinced to join the Moonies. I never thought it would affect our pizza order.

Let me explain. These summer nights, my youngest son, Lewis, plays for an AAA Little League team. That means that three or four times a week I go to the field to watch him goof around on the bench with other boys and stand in left field until it's too dark to see the ball. That also means that by the time we get home, my other two kids are gnawing on each other's flesh and there's no time to cook. On these nights, we order pizza.

Calling for a pizza is the no-brainer of being a mom. It's like dialing your lifeline on *Who Wants to Be a Millionaire?* And, frankly, this time of year I call that culinary lifeline a lot. In fact, on garbage day I sometimes hide the embarrassing empty pizza boxes in the neighbor's trash cans so no one will accuse me of being addicted to mozzarella or suspect me of having an affair with the delivery man.

I order pizza because it is one of the few food items that all three of my kids will eat (Pez and Marshmallow Fluff are the others) and because, if it's not nutritionally ideal, well, at least it's cheap and quick.

The problem is, my nonconformist kids feel compelled to express their individuality every chance they get—even when ordering pizza. Especially when ordering pizza. I guess this shouldn't come as a surprise. They can't agree on anything—not what radio station to listen to in the car, not what type of toothpaste we should buy and not what type of peanut butter goes best with marshmallow Fluff. So, it makes sense that they don't agree on what kind of pizza to order.

My oldest son, a purist, eats only plain cheese pizza. Lewis gags if there is any visible oregano and my daughter, an aspiring vegetarian, insists on the gastronomic travesty known as "The Hawaiian" They're not willing to compromise their pizza values, and I guess I should be proud of their conviction. But, they can't agree what to put on the pizza *or* where they want to order it from.

Our town has a plethora of pizza parlors (it's a classy place), but there's no one joint that can satisfy all of my mealtime mavericks. The shop that makes the best plain pizza doesn't do Hawaiian. The place that has pineapple uses lots of oregano and the pizza with no green specks in the sauce doesn't make the crust thin enough for my teenage gourmand. No matter where we get the pizzas, someone will complain and grumble all through dinner.

Maybe I should be proud that they are each wonderful in their own special way and celebrate my children's individuality. Or maybe we should order Chinese food, instead. Szechuan or Mandarin?

BLOOD SAUSAGE

I love to eat. I used to love to cook, too. But for the past two decades (Gee, that's how long I've had kids; what a coincidence!), I haven't cooked much at all. Oh, sure, I've browned chicken nuggets, sprinkled on cheese-flavored powder and dialed for pizza delivery, but rarely do I get to stretch my culinary muscles beyond macaroni or the microwave.

If it's not neon orange, my kids won't eat it—even something as simple as meatloaf or steamed broccoli will send them reeling with revulsion. They'll say: "This looks gross. This looks sickening. Can I have macaroni and cheese instead?"

Although I'm tired of the daily ritual of boiling water, my kids don't seem to care that their menu is maddeningly monotonous. The only time that they will try anything new is when they're invited to eat dinner at a friend's house. Then they come home and say "Why don't you ever make tripe? I had it at Victoria's was really good." Or "Mom, can you buy blood sausage next time you go to the store? Phillip's mom made it and it was great!"

So I buy it, I cook it and I serve it and my kids say, "It tasted better at Victoria's house," or "When Phil's mom made it, it was really good. This looks different. This looks gross. Can I have macaroni and cheese instead?"

I've asked other parents, "Did my son really eat cauliflower at your house?"

"Cleaned his plate and asked for seconds," they smugly report.

And that's not all. Not only are my kids gourmets at someone else's house, but these same kids—kids who have to be threatened before they will carry their plates to the sink, who eat macaroni and cheese with their hands and who think that napkins are only good for hiding vegetables that are too gross to eat or wadding up and throwing at your sister—are apparently transformed into paragons of gentility when they sit down to dinner at a friend's house. I have fielded reports that my kids are able to identify and employ both a fork and a knife, that they are capable of clearing their own dishes and that they even remember to say please when they ask for seconds of blood sausage.

But what really slays me are reports from the neighbors that my children actually contribute to dinnertime conversation. The same kid who, at home answers with a shrug when I inquire about his school day, cheerfully outlines entire lunchroom conversations and portions of classroom lectures when he is at someone else's dinner table. The same child whose idea of suppertime eloquence at home is belching the Pledge of Allegiance will go to a friend's house for dinner and debate the role of the presidency, discuss the threat of global warming and reveal that I bounced a check to the piano teacher.

I guess I should be glad that my children can muster up their manners when they are away from home. But just once, I'd like to be the one who gets to witness their sterling behavior and join them in a lively discourse over a plate of organ meat. Until that day, I'm accepting all dinner invitations on their behalf as well as recipes for blood sausage.

PLEASE PASS THE MANNERS

Q: Why does the turkey go "Gobble, gobble, gobble?"
A: Because he doesn't have good table manners.

Usually, I don't care how the food gets into my kids—as long as they eat. But last week, as my daughter entertained the family with a belched dinnertime rendition of *The Star Spangled Banner*, I decided that enough was enough. These kids need to learn some table manners.

After a summer of hamburgers, hot dogs and far too many nights of Chinese takeout, my kids have devised a hundred uses for disposable chopsticks, but are having real trouble telling the difference between a paper napkin and the bottom of their T-shirts. As my mother used to say, "What would they do if they were invited to Buckingham Palace?" By the look of things, they'd express their appreciation by burping out *God Save the Queen*.

However, while my family is not expecting to dine with royalty anytime soon, we are hosting a house full of relatives for Thanksgiving (including great aunts and uncles) who may not be impressed with my children's mealtime accompaniment or their creative use of chopsticks. I figured a few weeks should be plenty of time for my kids to brush up on their table manners and review the basic rules of civilization. I may have underestimated the task.

I know, I know, good manners should be used every day, and that if you only save them for special occasions, they get as dusty as your great aunt's soup tureen. But I'm hoping it's not too late to wipe off the Wedgewood and clean up our act. Frankly, I don't care if they know how to use a fish fork or finger bowl, but I would like them to be at least as well behaved as their cousins, who are also coming for Thanksgiving and who are—according to their mutual grandmother—perfect. I started by banishing belching and trying to replace it with appropriate dinner conversation.

"Did anything interesting happen to anyone at school today?" I asked around the table.

"At lunch Justin was imitating the teacher and I laughed so hard that milk came out of my nose," Lewis reported.

Obviously, there's room for improvement in the conversational realm. I made a list of topics to avoid at the table including: school lunches, descriptions of things that have come out of your nose, your friend's nose or any other orifice, jokes that involve the word "seafood" (as in "Do you like seafood?" followed by opening a mouth crammed with chewed up dinner and the charming witticism, "See? ... Food!"), scabs, the symptoms of Ebola, descriptions of what the dinner looks, smells or tastes like, and all non-verbal communication, including belching, gagging and humming.

Now that we had outlined appropriate conversation, it was time to tackle a dress rehearsal. The next night, we ate in the dining room, on the good china—with multiple forks, candles and cloth napkins—and it was just a Tuesday. But I felt like Helen Keller's teacher in the movie *The Miracle Worker.*

"Napkins on your laps!" I ordered as Lewis played matador with the dog. "No grabbing," I barked as my daughter knocked over her water in a rush to reach the last dinner roll.

"Sit!" I commanded as all three kids danced and twitched in front of their plates. As dinner progressed, my list of forbidden behaviors grew. No tilting in chairs, slithering under the table, talking to the dog or touching the person next to you. No shouting, "I claim the last roll!" or using forks to catapult pieces of meat, vegetables or other edible or non-edible objects across the room. No drumming, singing or playing with action figures at the table. No storing cooked vegetables in your cheeks and dashing off to the bathroom. No racing through dinner to get first dibs on the television. No clinking glasses with cutlery, gargling with milk or coating your fingers with candle wax and then peeling it off and leaving a mess under your plate.

"You mean we have to just sit here and eat?" Lewis asked incredulously. I looked at him and just had to laugh. Fortunately, I don't think anyone saw the milk come out of my nose.

DINNER PARTY DEBT

I love dinner parties—especially if they are at someone else's house. The only problem is that after you've gone to other people's houses and eaten their food, they expect to be invited to your house to eat your food.

It was with this sense of social obligation that two weeks ago, I called three other couples and invited them to come to our house for dinner. Tonight.

This morning, when the alarm went off, I knew I was already behind schedule. I should have been marinating the meat, chilling the wine and repainting the dining room. Instead, I nudged my sleeping husband and hissed, "Wake up! People are coming for dinner."

"Sweetie," he said as he rolled over, "it's seven o'clock in the morning."

"Actually," I said, "it's six-thirty, and there's a lot to do." I tied on my bathrobe and headed to the kitchen to make a list—even before I made coffee. Having a list would give me focus and help me calm down.

- Clean house
- Clean bathroom
- Clean fridge
- Shampoo carpets
- Check silverware for smudges and food bits
- Plan menu
- Shop for food
- Shop for wine
- Cook
- Wash dog
- Wash kids
- Reupholster couch
- Paint dining room
- Buy new napkins
- Buy new plates
- Buy new glasses

- Buy new tablecloth
- Buy new table
- Buy new house
- Move

This list didn't make me calm. It made me feel totally panicked and a little bit nauseous. Lewis wandered into the kitchen with two friends who had spent the night, and asked "Can we have pancakes?"

"No," I snapped. "Eat cereal and don't make a mess. We are having people over for dinner."

Maybe I should phone my guests and tell them that I'm sick, cancel the whole thing and rent a Clive Owen movie. Hmmmm … tempting, but cowardly.

Instead, I looked at the list and decided to concentrate my efforts on cleaning the bathroom. After all, it's the only room where the guests can really scrutinize your housecleaning or snoop in the medicine chest and discover your most embarrassing hygiene secrets. I didn't fill the medicine chest with marbles, but I did remove potentially incriminating items like Preparation H, Wart-Away and the Jolene bleach. Then I wiped the male territory around the toilet and spritzed the mirror with glass cleaner. I even scrubbed the tub with bleach and ammonia. The bathroom filled with deadly chlorine gas, but the rust stains in the tub remained.

So, I unscrewed the light bulb in the overhead fixture and placed a small candle on the back of the toilet. "Let 'em pee in the dark," I figured. "At least the bathroom smells clean."

I emerged from the toxic fog of cleaning products and checked the time. "It's one o'clock!" I announced to no one in particular. "The guests are coming in six hours! The guests are coming!" I galloped through the house like Paul Revere, picking up stray soccer balls, sweat socks, backpacks and other unsightly signs of family life and stashing them in the basement.

Then I recruited (okay, paid) my daughter to sprinkle baking soda on the rugs and vacuum, and asked (okay, paid) Lewis and his friends to sweep the front porch and check the silverware. I put my husband in charge of picking out appropriately adult music from our collection of CDs, which consist mostly of, *World of Warcraft*, Weird Al Yankovich and Microsoft Word Start-Up disks.

At three o'clock, I realized that there probably wasn't enough time to repaint the dining room; I needed to think about the food. So I logged on to Epicurious and looked through every cookbook on my kitchen shelf for inspiration and instruction.

"Don't fuss," my husband said. "Make something simple."

"There isn't enough time to fuss," I assured him as I dashed to the supermarket.

It was four-thirty when I got home. The guests were due at seven. I sautéed some sausage, dumped a couple of jars of spaghetti sauce into a pan and poured in a little red wine. Then I made a salad, wrapped some garlic bread in foil and poured a little more red wine for me.

At six-thirty, I wiped the kitchen counters, emptied the dishwasher and jumped into the shower. When the guests arrived, my hair was almost dry, the smell of sausages simmering had replaced the noxious chlorine gas fumes, and music—that wasn't Weird Al—was playing on the stereo.

By candlelight, my dining room didn't look like it needed repainting. It looked cozy; the silverware sparkled and you couldn't tell that the napkins weren't new. The spaghetti sauce passed as homemade, the conversation was lively and no one complained that they had to pee in the dark.

5

Elastic Waistland

A Household Word: Spinning

I know that aerobic exercise provides enormous cardio-vascular benefits. But I don't care about the shape of my left ventricle—I want thin thighs.

MOM JEANS

If you're like me, and still think that thongs are footwear, you probably don't wear low-rise jeans. You probably wear Mom Jeans. And, if you're like me, they make you look fat. That's what my teenage daughter says. She says that my faded jeans, the ones that button at the waist and taper at the ankle, are really unflattering. She says that hip-hugging, dark-rinsed, flared jeans are more slimming. Like anyone who weighs 103 pounds would know.

But the 103-pound youth market is who the fashion industry is courting. And who can blame them? My skinny kid is flush with babysitting money and has the stamina to beg me to drive her to the mall whenever a new issue of *Teen Vogue* or *Elle Girl* hits the stands. I, on the other hand, haven't bought a new pair of jeans in years.

That's because, for me, shopping for jeans is a traumatic experience. It's not just the three-way mirrors that reflect my doughy self-self-self in baggy underwear; it's finding jeans that fit. If they glide over my hips, the waist is huge. If the waist size is correct, I can't pull them up past my knees. They are always too long or the legs are too tight or they make me look fat. That's why I've been wearing the same jeans since the Clinton administration (Bill's, that is). I think of them as timeless classics.

"They're Mom Jeans," my daughter says. "They make your butt look big."

My daughter is nothing if not honest, so with her withering fashion commentary ringing in my ears, I donned a sweater long enough to cover the aforementioned region and we headed to the mall.

Going shopping with my teenage daughter is like hiking a small hill with a Nepalese Sherpa. You are in expert hands, but you don't necessarily speak the same language.

"Do you want flares, tapered or straight leg? Acid wash, sandblasted or dark wash? Low rise, super low rise, mid rise or curvy?" she asked, as we rifled through shelves of obsessively folded jeans in The Gap. I checked for a womanly size twelve lurking amid the twos, fours and zeroes. (What kind of size is zero?)

I looked for a price tag and remembered that a friend of mine once advised "Never worry about cost when you are buying jeans." Or was it when you're buying a bathing suit? Maybe it was life insurance. Anyway, I figured that if I found a pair of jeans that actually made my matronly posterior look smaller, it would be worth a little extra money ... heck, it would be priceless.

"Try the boot cut," my daughter shouted over the store's pulsating sound track. "They make your legs look longer."

"But I'll have to buy boots," I hollered back.

I finally found a pair that were my size and took them to the dressing room.

They were perfect. They weren't cut too low and the hems didn't drag on the ground. I thought they made my butt look okay and, best of all, they were comfortable. In these jeans, I'd be able to kneel down to pick up Legos off the living room floor and not worry about my underwear sticking out. I'd be able to reach up to the highest shelf in my kitchen without the rest of the family losing their appetite. I could even bend over to kiss my children as they sleep.

My daughter says I did it again—I got another pair of Mom Jeans, but I don't care. I have a mom body and Mom Jeans fit me just fine.

CONFESSIONS OF A CARBOHYDRIAC

There is nothing more boring than someone talking about their diet—except perhaps, someone writing about their diet. But I can't help it. I am on one of those trendy, high-protein, weight-loss plans and all I can think about is pizza, beer and empty carbohydrates. It's been three whole hours.

I chose the South Beach Diet because although it doesn't have the caché of being named for a dead physician, it does conjure up images of poolside cabanas and buff guys bearing trays of delectable tidbits. In reality, this diet is a metabolic boot camp where, for the first two weeks, your body transforms from burning glucose (which is sugar), into burning fat (which is your hips). That's the theory, anyhow.

It had better work, because aside from giving birth to three kids (who are directly to blame for my current, miserable shape), eliminating all bread, wine, chocolate, pasta and pleasure from my life has been the most difficult thing I've ever done.

The quest for a new me began when I woke up this morning and weighed myself. Naked, with an empty bladder, I held firmly onto the bathroom towel rack and stepped onto the scale—140 pounds. Ugh. I cut my fingernails and weighed myself again. No change.

Disgusted, I threw on a sweatshirt and a pair of jeans. It was a miracle! The waistband was loose and the jeans hung on my hips. Hallelujah! The diet works! I weighed myself again—141 pounds. I examined the jeans. They were my husband's. I pulled on sweatpants and headed downstairs to make breakfast for the kids.

I poured bowls of cereal and popped a few Frosted Flakes into my mouth. Then I remembered. Frosted Flakes are not allowed in Phase I of the South Beach Diet. They are made of corn, which is forbidden, and they are frosted with sugar, which is evil. They are also GRRRREEEEEAAAAT! I spat them into the sink.

"Mommy, what's wrong with the Frosted Flakes?" Lewis probed.

"Nothing," I lied. "It's just that they are loaded with carbohydrates and glucose and …"

"Actually, I don't think I want Frosted Flakes anymore," Lew said. "Can I have an Eggo instead?"

After the kids left for school, I ate the pieces of Eggo that were left floating in a pool of maple syrup and licked the plate clean. Hey, when I was a child, it was a sin to waste food. I repented for the waffle by making myself a breakfast straight from the South Beach Diet book:

- **6 oz. of tomato juice:** Ugh. Who's going to know if I have orange juice instead?
- **Scrambled eggs with fresh herbs and mushrooms:** The only mushrooms I found were growing on cheese in the back of the fridge, so I cracked an extra egg into the frying pan to compensate for the lack of fungi.
- **2 slices Canadian bacon:** Didn't I hear that you can eat unlimited bacon on this diet? I fried up four slices and didn't check Oscar Meyer's citizenship.
- **Decaf coffee with nonfat milk:** C'mon, I need caffeine to function—half and half, too.

I arranged the bacon and eggs on my plate. They looked lonely. One slice of toast (with a little butter and jelly) couldn't hurt.

I could almost feel the pounds melting away as I ate. I polished off the eggs, wiped the bacon grease off my lips and ran upstairs to check my progress—142 pounds. Something must be wrong. I had already been on the diet for over an hour. I took off my clothes, tightened my grip on the towel rack and adjusted the scale until it read 137. That's better. I slid back into my husband's jeans. This diet really does work. By lunchtime, I'll be able to celebrate the new me with a decent meal.

10,000 STEPS IN MY SHOES

I got a pedometer for Mother's Day and hadn't taken it out of the box. I had planned to walk from mid-May, all through the summer. Instead I told myself that I was getting plenty of exercise hanging around the shallow end of the town pool, yakking with the other moms and eating Fudgesicles, while the kids went off the high dive. Maybe the water just made me feel lighter. Anyhow, it was too hot to walk.

But now, summer's over and it's a new school year. Along with my resolution to ban video games until next June, I am also resolving to walk myself thin. Actually, I'd be happy to simply walk myself a little less fat. The brochure that came with the pedometer says that walking 10,000 steps a day will burn an extra 2,000-3,000 calories a week.

That's a lot of Fudgiscles.

Sure, there are aerobic benefits to walking, too. But frankly, I don't really care what my left ventricle looks like—as long as my thighs are thin.

The American Council on Exercise ranks the exertion level of various professions and reveals that while mail carriers rack up 19,000 steps every day, secretaries take only an average of 4,327 steps at work; restaurant employees walk about 10,000 steps and custodians beat waitresses with nearly 13,000 steps. I figure that my days most closely mirror those of a custodian or a restaurant worker so I must be logging the requisite 10,000 steps a day. Easy.

So, this morning, I clipped the pedometer to the waistband of my soon-to-be-a-size smaller jeans and started counting steps. I walked downstairs and made coffee (13 steps) trotted back upstairs to wake up my son Lewis (17 steps), went down to the basement to get clean laundry (21 steps), and then upstairs again to tell Lew to hurry up (15 steps). After breakfast, I ran a half block chasing Lewis with the lunch he left on the kitchen counter (52, steps), dashed through the house looking for my car keys (37 steps), went grocery shopping and powered through the produce section, meat department and frozen food section (227 steps). At home I made six separate trips carrying bags from the car to the kitchen (47 steps) and put away the groceries (4 steps). Then I went upstairs to retrieve my glasses from the bedside table (15 steps) and settled into work on the computer (0 steps). I also got up three times before lunch to let the dog out (18 steps). By noon, I had logged only a measly 466 steps. Only eight thousand, four hundred fifty eight steps to go.

The way I figure it, 10,000 steps is about five-miles, which is approximately eighty minutes of walking. Eighty-minutes! That's forty-minutes in each direction.

I tell you, if I ever got forty-minutes away from my house I might never turn back.

I was tempted to cheat on the 10,000 steps by strapping the pedometer to my ankle and shaking my foot while I watched Oprah and ate Fudgicles, or clipping it on the dog's collar and letting him chase the squirrels around the backyards. Who, I wondered, other than the mailman, has time to walk 10,000 steps? Not me. No wonder my jeans were still snug.

I needed to find a way to walk more. So, after school, when I brought Lewis and his friends to soccer practice, I also brought my pedometer and my sneakers and, instead of sitting on the sidelines with the other moms or going home to start dinner, I walked around and around and around the field. During the hour of practice, I circled the field twelve times, bringing my grand total to 6,493 steps—more than halfway to my 10,000-step goal. Only 3, 507 steps to go before bedtime.

But hey, who's counting?

Suits Me Fine

Okay, it's past Memorial Day. The mercury is climbing and soon I will be forced to peel off my black sweatpants and stuff myself into a swimsuit. It won't be pretty. I intended to be in fantastic shape for the annual unveiling of my thighs, but I didn't go to the gym and I didn't lock the fridge and I forgot to save up for liposuction. So now, my body is the shape and consistency of vanilla pudding. I blame it all on my kids. Before I had kids, I had the figure of a twenty-three year-old. Heck, I *was* a twenty-three year-old. This body is all their fault.

Before I had kids, I wore two-piece suits that proudly exposed my mid-section. Since I've been a mom, I've become the master of disguise. I wrap beach towels around my middle and cover my dietary transgressions with a voluminous black maternity suit. Nine years after my last pregnancy, the suit still evokes sympathetic stares and well-meaning questions.

"When's the baby due?"

"In 1995," I reply.

Now, after years of service, the elastic has disintegrated and the suit is baggy—even on me. It's time to toss the maternity suit and admit, before the *National Enquirer* starts getting interested, that I have not had a nine-year pregnancy. It's time to buy a new bathing suit.

I don't expect it to be easy—I have some tough criteria. I need a bathing suit that will minimize my figure flaws—a suit that will draw attention away from my deficits and accentuate my assets—one that's more burka than bikini. Price, naturally, is no object. If I found a bathing suit that made me look twenty pounds thinner and ten years younger, I would pay. A lot.

Oh sure, there are those "miracle" suits that are reinforced with steel and supposedly compress excess flesh to make you look pounds thinner, but I've looked at enough catalogs to be able to pick those suits out even on the most crowded beach. Whenever I see anyone wearing one, I automatically visualize ten, maybe even fifteen extra pounds. It makes me feel better about myself.

I've searched extensively for a new bathing suit. I've looked in the stores and I've shopped online. I've tried on thongs and sarongs, tankinis and one-piece racers, suits with skirts, suits with shorts, suits that promise to hold you in, push you up and flatten you out. I've tugged on suits that are designed to enhance your bust line, emphasize your waistline and eliminate your tan line. It has been torturous.

Believe me, there's nothing more loathsome than trying on bathing suits—except trying on bathing suits with a kid in the dressing room. Once, I brought my youngest child with me when I shopped for a swimsuit. My ego still hasn't recovered. He was full of questions. "How come your tummy sticks out? Why is your butt so big? Why do the bottoms of your arms move when you are standing still?"

There is just one answer: "Because I'm a mom."

MUST BE THE SHOES

Yesterday, a friend of mine brought me a pair of shoes. She had driven around with them in the trunk of her car for weeks. They were shoes that someone had given to her, but they were too small; they weren't her style. They were green Doc Martens. Some moms are cool; others have coolness foisted upon them.

"Those don't look like Mommy shoes," my youngest son, Lew observed as I took them out of the box.

"You're right," I told him. "They're not."

"They're good shoes," my friend said. "They're expensive. They've never been worn. Just try them on," she urged.

I did and they fit. Perfectly.

"They make your feet look like someone else's," Lew grumbled. He was right. I looked down. Those were not the feet of a sensible, suburban housewife. A mother of three wears tennis shoes with clean white socks or low-heeled pumps with knee-highs or clogs. These were the feet of an angry, young hipster. These feet should hang out in SoHo, not in the supermarket. These feet go to Lollapalooza, not to Little League. I didn't recognize my tame, size-seven tootsies anymore ... and I liked it.

All afternoon, I wore the shoes and, as I made lunches and drove the kids to playdates, I would glimpse at my feet and feel just a little hipper and just a tiny bit cool. I found my sunglasses and wore them as I chauffeured kids across town. I hung my arm out of the window and let the wind lick my hair. I wished that my minivan was transparent so that people could see that inside the standard-issue Mom-mobile was an edgy, way-cool, Doc Marten-wearing, woman who would not be shackled by suburbia.

I switched the car radio from the Disney station to alternative rock and cranked up the volume—just a little.

"Moooooommmmm!" Voices from the backseat protested the emergence of the new, hip mom.

"Mommy," Lewis whined after dinner, "Are you going to wear those shoes every day?"

"Lew," I said as I left for a PTO meeting, "I just might."

For the PTO, I paired the green Doc Martens with black jeans and a tan sweater. After the meeting, someone commented that I looked like I had lost weight. "Must be the shoes," I replied.

"Mom," my daughter Perry said today, "you're not actually going to wear those shoes again, are you? They make you look like you're in college."

"Sweetie," I replied, as I dashed in my Docs to drop off Lewis at a birthday party, "I may never take these babies off."

I never would have bought these shoes. I would never even have tried them on. I would have walked right past the whole display of clunky, nerd-chic, misunderstood, emo, footwear and gone straight to the mother-approved, sling backs, loafers and clogs. But, like the glass slipper in the fairy tale, the green Doc Martens were a perfect fit. And they were free.

I have always had a special affinity for a good deal. I don't like to spend a lot of money on clothes and I don't like to shop. I tend to buy the same beige sweaters and black pants over and over again. It's the same with shoes. My fashion motto has always been "try to blend in." But the new shoes have changed all that.

On my way home from the birthday party drop-off, I stopped into a store. There was a bright green shirt. It wasn't my style. It wasn't beige. Ordinarily, I wouldn't have given it a second look. It seemed like the kind of shirt that would appeal to someone who hangs out in SoHo; someone who wears Doc Martens. Cautiously, I brought it into the dressing room and scrutinized my reflection. The lime green matched my new shoes, made my hair look blonder and brought out the hazel in my eyes. Standing in the dressing room, I felt cooler, younger, and thinner. I bought the shirt and if anyone asks, I'll just say "It must be the shoes."

TAKE THREE TO FIVE

I went to the beauty parlor last week for a wash, cut and blow-dry. After the hair-dresser scrunched, spritzed and sprayed, I have to admit, my hair looked pretty good. The stylist handed me a mirror and while I was admiring the back of my head, he said "You should really use a deep conditioner on your hair to keep it healthy. Try this."

The bottle that he handed me looked like it had been designed by NASA. It was white and chrome and bullet-shaped. It was also tiny and cost twenty-two dollars. But my hair did look great and I was willing to try to keep it that way. "All you have to do," the stylist said, "is leave it on for three to five minutes."

"Whoa!" I said as I ran my fingers through my newly silken locks "Who has time to wait around in the shower that long?"

"Women with beautiful hair," he retorted as he rang up the bill.

"Not moms," I thought, "and not me." I've got three kids and no time for a beauty regimen. I keep all of my makeup (that would be my Chapstick) in my car and blow my hair dry by speeding to soccer games with the windows open.

In three minutes I can make school lunches, clean the bathroom for company, read the entire Sunday paper, attend a parent-teacher conference or have sex. Who knows what I could do with five minutes. Maybe I could create diamonds out of coal, grow a bonsai or get a full night's sleep. The twenty-two dollars I could manage, but finding three to five minutes would be tough.

At the dinner table that night, my new coif shone under the kitchen lamp. "How do you like the new me?" I asked. My husband and teenage son said that I looked the same. My daughter told me that I looked more normal (I think that's a compliment coming from a middle-schooler) and my youngest son, who is so opposed to change that he wears the same socks for a week said "I liked you better before."

Not me. I thought my hair looked great. It swung against my cheek as I loaded the dishwasher. It tickled my neck as I broke up a brawl between the boys and it still bounced while I did two loads of laundry, cleaned out the cat box, went through the kids' backpacks, took out the garbage and dashed out to the convenience store for a gallon of milk. When I collapsed in bed at midnight, my hair didn't. It was still shiny, swingy and, dare I say ... perky? It was Stepford hair and it was fabulous ... until the morning.

When I woke up, I rushed to the mirror and my shiny, blow-dried hair looked like bad topiary. It was fuzzy and stuck out at odd angles. "I'm taking a shower," I announced to my family. I closed the bathroom door, took off my watch and slipped the twenty-two dollar bottle of conditioner from its salon bag. The phone in the hall rang, there was a crash from the living room and I thought I heard someone call "*Mom!*" But when I turned on the shower, all I heard was the sound of rushing water. I poured the supermarket brand shampoo into my hand and worked the lather through my hair. I rinsed. I repeated. Then, I reached for the tiny twenty-two dollar bottle.

Four minutes, I vowed. I will leave the conditioner on for four minutes. I uncapped the bottle and the heady scent of herbs and citrus filled the shower stall. I squeezed a tiny blob onto my palm and rubbed it on my head. Then I waited, and waited, and waited. I tried to mediate and inhale the twenty-two dollar aroma (twelve seconds), I shaved my legs (thirty-five seconds), I examined my fingernails (two seconds) and I practiced holding in my stomach (eleven seconds). I checked the time. I still had three more minutes of conditioning. I felt like I was wasting water, so I turned off the shower. I thought about productive things that I could do naked in the tub with conditioner on my head. I could regrout the tile, scrub the inside of the tub or practice Kegel exercises. Or I could just rinse the stuff off and go out and referee the chaos that I could now hear mounting in the living room. Instead I turned the shower back on and for three full minutes, I did absolutely nothing. I simply closed my eyes and enjoyed every fragrant moment of the wait.

Now, my hair doesn't look as good as it did the day I left the salon, so I guess the conditioner isn't magical—just expensive. I'll keep using it though, because twenty-two dollars for three to five minutes of peace and quiet seems like a bargain.

6

The Breakdown Lane

A Household Word: **Overtime**

The way I see it, my job as a parent is to put myself out of business. So far, I've got job security.

DIRTY SOCKS AND CARBON FOOTPRINTS

Global warming is probably the most serious issue affecting our planet. Although I suspect if we all simply stopped driving our kids to soccer, the Earth would plummet into another Ice Age. So this spring, in addition to boycotting my son's away games, I'm taking additional steps to reduce carbon emissions, conserve energy and keep the ice caps intact. I figure that if I reduce my family's impact on the Earth, not only will I help the environment; I might even improve my own quality of life.

In my quest for carbon neutrality, I've decided to stop vacuuming. Turns out, a canister vacuum like mine sucks up a whopping 800 watts of electricity per month. Now, the cat hair on the couch and the dust bunnies under the dining room table can provide extra insulation as well as visible proof that I am doing my part for the planet. When company comes, I'll just unscrew our fluorescent bulbs (more energy savings!) and light a candle. I'm sure my guests will appreciate the ambience.

With the time I save by not vacuuming, I can relax and watch television (which consumes a mere 180 watts a month). Who knew that tuning into *Oprah* and the *Food Network* could help stave off global warming?

To further reduce my family's carbon footprint, I've also cut way back on how frequently I do laundry. After all, in a month of average use (and my family is way above average) the washing machine drains about 15,000 gallons of potable water, as well as more than 600 watts of electricity. And the dryer burns up a staggering 13,000 watts.

So when the kids complain "Moooommmmm, I don't have any clean socks!" I just say, "Turn them inside out and they'll be good for another week." Same goes for underwear. I know Al Gore would approve and I feel good about treading lightly (albeit in dirty knee-highs) on the Earth.

Deforestation is also contributing to climate change. We all know that saving paper can save trees. So, in the spirit of environmental consciousness, I've replaced the rolls of squeezable Charmin in my kids' bathroom with those little, gray, scratchy sheets that they have at highway rest stops. I lost the ability to control their toilet paper consumption when they stopped demanding "Wipe me!" Now, unsupervised, they gaily unfurl yards of the stuff at each sitting. I know—because I'm the only one whoever replaces the empty rolls, and I replace them frequently. The result of this ticker-tape mentality has resulted in clear cutting in Brazil and clogged drains in my bathroom. Maybe the little scratchy sheets will make using toilet paper a little less of a celebratory occasion and more of an opportunity to meditate on the importance of trees. Maybe I should put a basket of oak leaves next to the toilet.

Perhaps the most significant step I've taken to stop global warming is to cut my consumption of gasoline. I've radically reduced the number of unnecessary car trips to places like ... the supermarket.

The way I see it, if we're out of milk, the kids can drink water. If we're out of food we can get take-out. Ordering Chinese food or pizza saves some of the 12,500 watts that the stove uses during an average month and, because the delivery guy's out there driving around anyway, I figure he might as well stop at my house. When I do cook, I try to use the microwave (only 1,300 watts!) instead of the range. That means when the kids ask, "What's for dinner?" the answer is popcorn.

I feel good that my family is doing more to help protect our planet. Personally, I think laying off the housework can really make a difference. The way I figure it, sometimes doing more means doing way less—and that's a sacrifice I am willing to make.

MOM SHOOTS AND MISSES

Paper snowflakes hang on the auditorium stage. The pianist shuffles through her sheet music and the parents jockey for prime positions with video cameras poised, zoom lenses focused and flash batteries freshly charged.

It's the Winter Concert, formerly known as the Holiday Concert and once upon a time called the Christmas Concert. The accompanist pounds out the opening chords of "Frosty the Snowman" and the children file down the center aisle and take their place on stage. The kindergarteners are solemn in velvet jumpers and tiny bow ties. The skinny legs of sixth-grade girls are sporting their first pantyhose and the boys' hair is spiked with gel. My son is here too, looking like a waiter, in a white shirt and new black pants.

As the kids walk by, parents push like paparazzi into the aisle to snap photos. I dig in my purse for my camera, but the Kodak moment is fleeting and by the time the little green light signals that the flash is ready, Lewis has disappeared into the sea of sixth-grade heads. Shoot, I mean darn! Another moment remains unrecorded for posterity.

It's not the first time that I have missed the shot. Although I fully intend to take pictures of the momentous occasions in my children's lives, it just doesn't happen. It's certainly not for lack of photographic equipment. We have plenty of cameras in our house. There are disposable cameras that have gone through the wash with the kid's camp laundry, thirty-five millimeter cameras that need batteries or are out of film, a digital camera with no more room on the memory card and a video camera that came with a million cables and attachments, but no instruction booklet. There's even a camera on my cell phone—but the only one who knows how to take pictures with it is Lewis, and he uses his photographic expertise to document the neighbor's dog and the inside of his own mouth.

When I do find a camera that works, I leave it on the hallway table (where I put it so I wouldn't forget it) or I accidentally hit rewind or I forget to buy batteries. From birthday parties to bar mitzvahs, the excuses are different, but the results are always the same. No photos.

Sure, we have baby pictures of our first child. Fortunately, all ultrasounds look alike, so each of our subsequent children remains convinced that they are the fuzzy bean-shaped blob.

Over the years, other parents at soccer games and school plays have taken pity on me and have given me copies of their photos. So, now I have lots of snapshots that feature other people's children—with my kid playing a supporting role. There's Barbara's daughter in the kindergarten play with half of my daughter visible to her left. There's Scott's kid scoring a goal and I think that's the back of Lewis' jersey.

Frankly, I'm a little envious of those families who take pictures. Already this year we've received Christmas ... err, I mean holiday cards from the photographically inclined. These are people who are able to assemble their entire family in front of the hearth in August and get them to smile while wearing matching reindeer sweaters. They even get the dog to smile. Some of these portraits were taken by professionals. I can tell.

We've had professional photographers capture our family on film, too. I spent twelve dollars for a photo of us screaming on the SooperDooperLooper at Hershey Park. You can see my tonsils. There's another of us drenched in blue ponchos on the log flume ride. We even have a photo of us singing with Elvis at Madame Tussaud's Wax Museum. While none of these shots are very flattering, I like to believe that future generations will think that we lived in exciting times—certainly more exciting than the Winter Concert.

My son is in the third row and, while I can't see his new black pants, I can see that he looks totally bored. Frankly, I don't think that he is even moving his lips. Still, I know that even if you don't take pictures, children grow up in a flash. So, if anyone at the Winter Concert has a photo of my kid—I'd like a copy.

NO, NO NINTENDO!*

It's December. That means that it's prime time for my ten-year-old son to remind me what he wants for Christmas (a Nintendo), for Hanukkah (a Nintendo), for his half birthday (a Nintendo) and as a reward for finishing his supper (a Nintendo).

When I was ten, I begged my parents for a pony, but times have changed and gifts of livestock don't hold the same appeal for this generation. My son wants electronics. My son wants Nintendo.

According to Lewis, he's the only kid in town, quite possibly the only child in all of America, that doesn't have a Nintendo game system. And it's not fair. This makes our house really boring and makes me a serious contender for the Joan Crawford Motherhood Award.

The way my son sees it, depriving him of a Nintendo is tantamount to withholding food or forcing him into hard labor. It's practically child abuse and it's just not fair. Besides, everybody else has one.

"Please Mom," he begs. "I'll even pay for it with my own money."

But, as I have explained to him during the weeks preceding other gift-giving holidays, money isn't the issue—even if he could save enough dollar bills from the Tooth Fairy. I know Nintendo doesn't cost a fortune—our family easily spends the equivalent on stuff like ski lift tickets, Girl Scout cookies or a dinner out. It's the mind-numbing, sit-on-your-butt, seizure-inducing lack of creativity that makes me want to embrace a more Amish lifestyle.

"Lewis," I sigh. "If they were giving away Nintendo at Toys 'R Us, I would say, 'No thanks' and head straight to the Legos."

"How about if I get all A's on my report card?" he asks hopefully. "Then can I get a Nintendo?"

Somehow, rewarding academic achievement by encouraging *Mario Party* doesn't seem right. And, if he doesn't get stellar grades, I don't want him playing *Super Monkey Ball* when he could be reading, reviewing his multiplication tables or developing cold fusion.

Besides, having one more thing in our house that I have to monitor, regulate and negotiate about will drive me over the edge. I'm already nagging my kids to turn off the television, log off the computer and hang up the phone so that they can finish their homework, clean their rooms and practice saxophone. I don't need to add Nintendo to the mix.

Families who do have Nintendo argue that their kids hardly ever play it. If that's the case, I don't see why I should spring for one. Come to think of it, I've never heard any parent say, "We're so glad that we bought little Tyler a Nintendo. *Luigi's Mansion* has been such an *enriching* experience."

Sure, it would be easy to make my son happy this holiday season. I could just break down and buy the Nintendo Game Cube and the game cartridges, or I could attempt to develop his character with the gift of disappointment.

Yesterday, as I drove a herd of fifth-graders to music lessons, one little girl queried the group: "Do you believe in Santa?"

The kids murmured mixed replies. Some wavered on the verge of disbelief, others were still fervent in their faith. Then my son spoke up: "If I get a Nintendo for Christmas, I'll know that Santa's real. My parents will never buy one for me."

He's right. but I'm willing to discuss a pony.

*Disclaimer: I eventually caved on this issue (see *Wii Wish You a Merry Christmas*) and we now own a Wii and an Xbox 360. Who knew that I would rule at Guitar Hero?

MEALS ON WHEELS

The kid just stood there. He wouldn't get into the backseat of my car with the other seven-year-old soccer players.

"Get in," I admonished.

"I can't," he said. "The seat has crumbs on it."

I whacked at the crumbs with a road map. "Who do you think you are," I asked, "Howard Hughes?" He stared at me blankly, then opened his backpack, took out his windbreaker and spread it on the seat to protect himself from any contaminants that might still be lurking in the upholstery. He cast a doubtful look at me as he edged tentatively onto the backseat.

"Why is your car so messy?" he asked.

I have to admit that my car is a disaster area. I blame it on my kids. If I weren't a mom, there wouldn't be seven linty pacifiers, two dead bananas and a decapitated X-Man figure under the driver's seat of my minivan. If I weren't a mom, my car would be clean. I'd have a cute little litter bag to hold an occasional tissue instead of the big black Hefty bags that I seem to fill up almost daily.

I wanted to take the little neat freak and tell him all about kids and car pools and drive-through McDonald's. I wanted to ask him how come the same kid that comes to my house and smears grape jelly on the guest towels in the bathroom is squeamish about getting into a car that's got a couple Cheez-Its ground into the floor mats?

"My mother doesn't let us make crumbs in the car," another child piped up from the rear as I passed a bag of pretzel sticks to the backseat.

"*Hate her,*" I thought.

Oh sure, when the minivan was brand new, I was determined to keep it crumb-free. I made the kids take off their shoes, spit out their chewing gum and empty their pockets before they climbed into the backseat. That was on the way home from the dealership. Since then, in order to preserve my sanity and my family's quasi-dysfunctional lifestyle, I've had to relax my cleanliness standards.

Frankly, shuttling three kids around town to piano lessons, soccer practice and scout field trips means that the car is our second home. Okay, maybe it's more like a second kitchen. In fact, if I didn't let my kids eat in the car, I don't think that they would eat anything at all. All I know is that my kid, who refuses to eat lunch in the kitchen before we drive to the supermarket, is guaranteed to be ravenous the minute the car key is in the ignition.

We eat our meals on the way to school, to soccer and to scouts. I also use car snacks as all-occasion bribery. "Come shoe shopping and we can stop and get an ice-cream cone to eat on the way home" or "Don't complain on the way to the doctor's office and you can bring a bag of popcorn (the cardinal sin of auto-snacking) with you." As long as the snacks hold out, the kids are reasonably cooperative.

For longer trips, snacks are a necessity. Our minivan doesn't have a CD player, a DVD player or even a very good radio. The only entertainment available in the backseat is fighting or eating. My kids fight less when their mouths are full. And who knows, the moldy apple cores under the driver's seat and the stale Cheerios that have worked their way into every crevice of the dashboard could be our salvation if we are ever stranded in a snowstorm in the Dakotas or broken down in Death Valley. The way I figure it, if people weren't supposed to eat in the car, God wouldn't have made cup holders.

We're planning to drive four hours to visit relatives over Thanksgiving. To preserve the peace during the trip, I'll pack plenty of crackers, mozzarella sticks, animal crackers, apples, graham crackers, bananas and Chips Ahoy. I'm sure that my sister-in-law will understand when she passes the platter of turkey around and my kids shake their heads and say, "No thanks, we already ate in the car."

MY SINK RUNNETH OVER

"Mom! The sink is overflowing!"

I race to the kitchen and switch on the disposal: Click. Nothing.

Maybe it was the remnants of the shrimp cocktail that I made for New Year's Eve, or the peels from the Thanksgiving sweet potatoes, or a bamboo skewer that inadvertently ended up in the sink after the Labor Day cookout. Heck, in my house it could even be Legos or the television remote or my prescription sunglasses. Whatever it was, it made the garbage disposal back up, break down and die. My daughter commented that years of ingesting my cooking had finally killed it.

I confess, I'm not a great cook. But in our family, I am the only cook. So after preparing three meals a day, seven days a week, for five people, for eighteen years, when the kitchen appliances go on the fritz, I don't blame them. In fact, I feel sympathetic. I also feel like going out to eat. I figure we all deserve a break.

When I do cook, in order to compensate for my mediocre culinary skills, I use a lot of dishes. This morning I made breakfast and now the sink is overflowing with plates and mugs and greasy gray water where knives lurk like gators in the Everglades.

I'd put my head down and cry, but there's no counter space, just dirty dishes. So, I don rubber gloves and troll the murky depths of the sink for silverware then load the coffee mugs and egg-encrusted pans into the dishwasher and hit the *Heavy Duty* cycle. As part of an apparent suicide pact, the dishwasher makes a sympathetic grinding noise, belches more filthy water up into the sink and emits the faint odor of burning rubber.

"Hey, I smell something cooking!" my teenage son says as he bounds into the kitchen. "What's for dinner?"

"Pizza or Chinese," I say as I hand him a stack of take-out menus.

"Sa-we-eeet!" he breathes.

Now, my approach to appliance repair is to ignore the problem and seize the opportunity to go out to eat. I like to believe that whatever's wrong is just a temporary situation that's probably caused by sun spots or by bad karma, and that it will eventually go away. If it doesn't, well, at least I'll have had a decent meal.

My husband lacks my faith in the ability of inanimate objects to heal themselves. He views our quarter acre of suburbia as a battleground. It's us against the crabgrass, the neighbors and the appliances. He is confident that, properly armed, he will emerge victorious. Today, he meets the enemy head-on with a can of Drano and a coat hanger.

"I told you not to put shrimp into the disposal," he mutters as he bends the hanger into the shape of Florida and shoves it into the sludge in the sink.

"It's called the In-Sink-Erator," I retort. "It should be able to handle a few measly shrimp."

It's not that I don't have confidence in my husband's abilities as a handyman, I do. He has replaced broken windows, repaired the front steps and re-grouted bathroom tile. But, as he sinks elbow deep into the fetid water, I see a telltale vein bulge in his temple and I know that we need more than a coat hanger. We need professional help.

I open the Yellow Pages and look for a plumber—preferably one with experience as a marriage counselor. But frankly, I don't think our problem is anything that a nice dinner out can't fix.

TAKE ME TO THE RIVER

Yesterday, while I was in my basement contemplating a mound of dirty laundry, I found some old *National Geographic* magazines. Instead of sorting the whites and the colors, I became engrossed in the pictures. In one issue, there was a photo essay on caves (which looked a lot like my basement laundry room, only sunnier). Another had pictures of women washing their clothes in a river. Ugh, I thought, I'm glad I don't live there! There are probably crocodiles in that water.

Then I looked at the picture again. The sun was shining on the river. The women were smiling and talking to each other. Some were even laughing. I never laugh when I do the laundry.

Laundry is my least favorite chore. Maybe I hate it because I always end up with a pile of mismatched socks. Or maybe I dread doing the laundry because my washer and dryer are in the basement, wedged between my husband's tools, rusty tricycles and those old magazines. It's dark down there ... lonely, too. I usually avoid doing the wash until my family runs out of clean underwear. "Wear your bathing suits under your clothes," I tell my kids. "I'll do the laundry later today."

That's why I was staring at a mountain of dirty clothes that perfectly preserved my family's not-so-recent fabric history. At the bottom were nearly petrified beach towels from our trip to the beach last summer. Next, came a fetid sediment of soccer pads and knee socks from the fall season. The strata continued with a layer of linty fleece tops. Dingy underwear and mismatched socks from yesterday crowned the peak. It was a grubby monument to the merits of nudism.

I examined the picture of the women at the river again. They don't have their own washers with a special cycle for lingerie. They don't have dryer sheets, fabric softener or color-safe bleach. Heck, they don't even have plumbing. All they have is water, rocks, sunshine and each other. Sure, my Maytag might get clothes a little cleaner, but I think I'd be willing to sacrifice a few shades of white for a laugh with friends on laundry day. Besides, I could blame the missing socks on the crocodiles.

I imagined the women on my street, washing load after load of laundry alone in their dark basements. Somehow, the women at the river bank seemed far less primitive.

I thought about my town. There is no river, and besides, there must be all sorts of wetlands regulations that would prohibit public laundering. Then I had an idea.

I called my neighbor Denise and asked, "Do you have a pile of laundry in your basement?"

"Do I ever!" she said. "It's creeping up the basement stairs. It scares me."

"Get it," I ordered as I held the phone with my chin and stuffed my own composting clothing into big black trash bags.

We loaded our dirty laundry into the trunk of my car and headed for the Laundromat. Together, we separated whites and colors, added detergent and loaded quarters into eight machines. While the washers chugged, we drank coffee, talked and even had a couple of laughs. It wasn't the river, but it was better than being alone in the basement. Next week, we're going to take our laundry to the fountain at the mall. Hope there aren't any crocodiles.

7

Chairman of the Bored

A Household Word: **Bedtime**

Take two kids who have spent all afternoon arguing over Xbox, whacking each other with sticks in the back yard and calling each other "fart face," tell them it's time to go to their respective homes, and you can bet they'll say, "Can we have a sleepover?"

CEREAL MOM

My kids love going on vacation. It's not because we travel to glamorous locations (like Lake Winnipesauke or my mother's house) or because they enjoy being scrunched in the back seat of the station wagon for hours. No, the reason my kids love family vacations is because they get to eat sugary cereal. This is, apparently, the highlight of their young lives.

During the school year, I am mean and only buy organic, whole-grain, no-nonsense, high-fiber, low-sugar cereal from Whole Foods. But, before we load up the car for a summer vacation, I take temporary leave of my senses and let the kids loose in the supermarket where they can pick out a box of their own artificially-colored, chemically-flavored, marshmallow-studded, sugar-coated, tooth-rotting cereal—the kinds that are advertised on television. Oh, happy day!

Which cereal to pick is a huge decision that prompts much debate in the aisles of the Foodmaster Supermarket. Each brand must be carefully evaluated. Are the pieces a cool shape or are they just flakes? Will they turn the milk blue and pink? Is there a free sticker inside the box? Can you win a prize by sending in the proof of purchase? There's the lure of the Snak-Pak, which offers variety over quantity, and there's the risk of investing in a glamorous new cereal and getting stuck with an entire box of something that looked great on television, but tastes gross. There is competition, intense concentration and huge stakes riding on each child's ultimate choice. My children do not seek my opinion as they weigh their options, and I do not offer advice. I define the parameters of the purchase, then lurk around the produce department and pretend that I'm not their mother.

Here are the rules of Vacation Cereal:

1. You can eat your vacation cereal as much as you want. Have it for breakfast, have it for snacks—you can even have it for lunch and dinner—until it runs out.

2. One box per child and one box only; the standard twelve to sixteen ounce size. No exceptions (except for the Snak-Pak). When it's gone, you cannot ask to share your siblings' box of cereal. But, if they offer to share, you may accept.

3. Trading bowls of cereal is permitted.

4. Milk is required on all cereal being consumed as a meal. Dry cereal is acceptable for snacks only.

5.   Prizes, proofs of purchase and other promotional materials are the property of the child who has selected that particular box of cereal.

The cereal is, I'm convinced, the only aspect of our trips that my kids care about. In fact, cereal is the only thing that they remember about our family vacations. "Remember when we took the boat under Niagara Falls last summer?" I ask my youngest son.

"Was that where I had Lucky Charms?"

This year, as I planned our summer vacation, I asked for input from the kids. "I thought it might be fun to spend some time doing a little rooftop tarring in Alabama or hiking through Death Valley or attending a conference on Tax Accounting in Houston," I ventured. "What do you guys think?"

They considered the vacation options then said, "Can we get cereal?"

CAMP IS IN-TENTS

It was getting late. Most of the other parents had already said their goodbyes and were headed home. Boys were starting to settle in, claiming the best bunks, unpacking their duffle bags and whacking tether balls while they waited for the swim test. But not my son.

It was Nathan's first time at camp. A week in the woods with no mommy had seemed like a good idea when we signed up and paid the deposit in February. Now, he leaned against a tree and looked miserable.

"We can't leave," I whispered to my husband, "He looks too sad."

Nathan's best friend, Dylan, was supposed to be there. They were going to bunk in the same tent, sign up for the same activities and together vowed to not bathe for the whole week. But, as we were loading the car with my son's sleeping bag, backpack and Ninja Turtle pillow the phone rang. It was Dylan, who, whether actually sick or merely suffering from cold feet, said he wasn't going to go to camp.

"Whaddaya mean you're not going?" I barked into the receiver. "Let me talk to your mother."

"What can I do?" Dylan's mother said. "He doesn't want to go."

I wanted to throttle him. I wanted to throttle her. I was furious. How could they do this to my kid?

"That's okay," my son said. "I still want to go."

"You do?" I was surprised, proud and frankly, a little worried.

I thought of my kid alone and friendless for one whole week at camp. Then I thought of the nonrefundable deposit, the cancellation fees, the already-loaded minivan and the prospect of him moping around for the house for seven days.

"Great," I said. "You'll make new friends. Let's go."

Nathan was quiet in the backseat as we drove along the highway.

"Are you excited?" I asked as we pulled onto the gravel road that led to the camp.

"Kinda" he replied.

We unloaded his gear, handed in the health forms and got in line for the head lice check. After my son was declared bug free, we brought his stuff to his tent, checked out the canoes at the lake, and walked to the archery range.

"Wow, this looks great," I gushed. Nathan shrugged.

We stayed for the hot dog lunch and lingered, waiting for our son to show some enthusiasm about being at camp. But he just looked unhappy.

"Maybe we should just take him home," I suggested to my husband. "Maybe this whole camp thing was a bad idea."

"Let's wait a few more minutes," he said. "Maybe he'll perk up."

We sat at the picnic table and watched Nathan kick at the dirt with the toe of his sneaker. What was I thinking? He was only nine years-old. There was no reason that he had to spend a week in the woods without electricity, indoor plumbing or me.

With each minute, he looked more miserable. We tried not to hover. We tried not to notice the hurt look in his eyes as he glanced over to where we were waiting for him to join in a game, to crack a smile, to give us some sign that he'd be okay.

I cornered a counselor, the camp director and the camp nurse. They all assured us that our son would adjust.

"Just say goodbye," said the nurse. "He'll be fine."

"Swim test starts at three o'clock," the counselor said. "Parents are usually gone by then."

"Maybe we should talk to him," I said to my husband. "Maybe we should take him home." Nathan was standing a few feet away, picking at the bark of a tree. He looked like he was about to cry. My heart ached for the little guy. I wanted to whisk him out of the woods and take him home to bask in the glow of the television set.

"What's the matter, Sweetie?" I asked tenderly.

He looked at me with tears welling up in his eyes and said, "Aren't you guys ever going to leave?" And so we did.

LEMONADE STANDARDS

It was quiet in my house. The dog was sleeping, my daughter was at day camp and my son Lewis, and his friend, Will, were in the basement playing video games. I should have poured myself a glass of iced tea and stretched out on a chaise lounge. Instead, I made the boys turn off the television.

"Go play outside!" I yelled from upstairs. This is my mantra every summer and I repeat it often. Moments later, I heard them in the kitchen rummaging through the cabinets, opening the fridge and rooting through the pantry. I went to investigate.

Every wineglass and water goblet was lined up on the counter; ice cubes were melting on the table and the kitchen looked like it had been ransacked by raccoons. Maybe video games aren't so bad.

"We want to have a lemonade stand," my son said. "Can you take us to get supplies?" Impressed by their entrepreneurial spirit and pleased that they actually did turn off the TV; I agreed that if they cleaned up, I would drive them to the supermarket.

At the store, I fork over ten dollars. They trot across the parking lot and in moments, return with two cans of powdered lemonade-flavored drink mix, a tower of paper cups and $3.47 in change.

"Mom!" Lewis says, as he hands over the change, "Did you know that this is enough to rent *Revenge of the Sith*?" I pull into the driveway and the boys race into the house. By the time I get to the kitchen, they have already emptied a plastic container of dry dog food and filled it with tap water and scoops of lemonade-flavored mix.

"Taste this," Lewis says, as he hands me a half cup of lukewarm, pink stuff. I try to ignore the floating particles of kibble and take a sip.

"Needs ice," I say.

They plop a tray of ice cubes into the lemonade and it overflows onto the counter and cascades onto the floor. But it's nothing an entire roll of paper towels can't absorb.

"If we sell all of this lemonade," Will says, eyeing the former dog food container, "we'll be able to *buy 'Revenge of the Sith.'*"

"How much are you going to charge?" I ask.

"Umm, twenty-five cents," says Lewis.

"Fifty," counters Will.

"Whoa! A dollar a cup. Then we won't need to sell as much," my kid says, displaying some real business acumen.

"Maybe you should donate part of the money you make to a good cause," I suggest. "Like saving the whales or ending global warming. You might even sell more that way."

A glimmer of interest flickers in their eyes. "Nah," they say. They swipe four sheets of paper from the computer printer and make signs that say:

"Lemonaid 25¢." They are in a hurry to earn big bucks and can't be bothered with stuff like spelling or rinsing out dog food containers.

"Mom, can we bring the coffee table outside?"

"Can we use the couch cushions?"

"Do you have something that we can put our money in?"

"Can I take the spare change out of your wallet?"

I am tempted to send them back into the basement and tell them to turn on the television, but instead I drag a card table and two folding chairs out of the garage, evict a pair of dressy pumps from a shoebox in my closet and hand over the $3.47 from my wallet.

"If we do buy *Revenge of the Sith*, I get to keep it 'cause I have an Xbox," says Lewis. "No fair!" says Will.

They argue about where to hang the signs, about who will pour and about how to spend their profit. But it is all moot because the neighborhood is deserted and business isn't exactly booming.

The boys take turns hollering down the empty street, drinking the lemonade and crushing the empty cups against their foreheads. I spy from behind the living room curtains to make sure that they are not approached by felons or abducted by aliens. Once in a while, I go outside, hand over twenty-five cents, bring the cup into the kitchen and pour the lemonade down the drain. I figure it's a small price to pay to keep them out of the house.

ENDLESS SUMMER

I love summer. It's school vacation that I can't stand. My kids have been out of school since June. That's seven weeks of Popsicle-stick crafts and whining to watch television. The kids may be bored, but I'm certifiable.

Seven weeks ago, I was full of ideas for fun outings and warm and fuzzy family bonding experiences. I planned to help the kids construct a lemonade stand so that they could experience the thrill of entrepreneurship and learn the value of a dollar. I wanted to show them how to catch fireflies at dusk and watch as they toasted marshmallows to golden-brown over the backyard grill. I pictured them dashing through the sprinkler while I sipped iced tea in the shade. There would be no time for cartoons or mindless computer games. We would carpe every diem of the whole damn summer.

But by July, things started to go awry. We ran out of lemonade mix and discovered that the only bugs that come out at dusk in our neighborhood are mosquitoes. My seven-year old dumped the plastic bag full of marshmallows into the barbecue and caused a toxic meltdown over the gas jets. The town's ban on lawn watering shut down the sprinkler. To cope, I turned on the television and let my kids watch Scooby Doo in the middle of a perfectly beautiful afternoon.

Now it's August, and I've had enough. I need a break from filling water balloons and fetching Frisbees from the roof. Summer vacation is exhausting and I'm using the Popsicle sticks to count the hours left until school starts. Frankly, I am on the edge and don't know if I can cling onto my sanity until September. Here are the warning signs that you too may be reaching your limit of summer fun.

The Top Ten Signs that You are Ready for School to Start

10. The lunch boxes are packed. Salmonella ... bah!
9. You miss the sense of foreboding you used to feel at 2:45 every afternoon.
8. You've replaced reading aloud from Harry Potter with reading aloud from back-to-school flyers.
7. It's okay that the school bus driver was on "America's Most Wanted."
6. "I don't care if it's still light outside. You're going to bed!"
5. You've gained five pounds since you stopped running after the school bus.
4. You're hoarding shoe boxes for the third-grade diorama project.
3. You agree that ketchup is a vegetable.

2. You're beginning to think that playground bullies might build character.

1. You have romantic dreams involving the principal.

If you exhibit one or more of these symptoms, call your school department and demand that they adopt a longer school year, or that they at least reimburse you for the craft materials and the Zantac. Tell them that although there's no evidence of superior academic achievement in children who go to school in August, their mothers are likely to be more mentally stable—probably because they haven't tried to make a birdhouse out of popsicle sticks.

REDEFINING LABOR DAY

My kids hate Labor Day. For them, the long weekend means the end of carefree, summer days spent hanging around the house and the beginning of days spent at school. I guess that's why it has become one of my favorite holidays.

Yesterday, as I flipped the pages of the kitchen calendar from August to September, I was giddy with excitement. "Look," I said trying to mask the glee in my voice. "You kids go back to school right after Labor Day!"

"What *is* Labor Day, anyway?" Lewis, asked. I wanted to lie and say that it's a day of mandatory and complete silence to honor the mothers who have resisted eating their young. But instead, I seized another opportunity.

"It's a day when parents get to rest and kids do all the work," I lied.

"Really?" he wondered.

"Yes, and I have lots of fun chores planned for you and your brother and sister."

Chores. I just love that word. It conjures up images of freckle-faced kids cheerfully gathering eggs and mowing lawns. It's a word I associate with Opie, Wally and the Beaver—not with my kids. Frankly, my kids' idea of hard work is buttering their own toast.

Believe me; I've tried to get them to pitch in. I've created chore charts and job wheels and matrixes. I've instituted reward systems with stickers, coupons and cold, hard cash. I've nagged and bribed and threatened and yelled. I'm not asking my kids to tar the roof or rebuild the transmission in the minivan. I'm only asking them to pick up the Legos off the floor and keep a clear path from the bedroom door to their beds. Heck, I'd be happy if they'd just remember to flush the toilet. "Sweetie," I say to my daughter, "would you please pick up the seventeen damp bath towels that are molding on your bedroom floor?"

"I'll do it later," she says, meaning when she goes away to college.

So, I end up picking up her towels, putting away my son's Legos and flushing the toilets myself.

According to the experts, I'm not doing my kids any favors. They say that chores build character and that kids who help around the house perform better in school, have healthier relationships with other members of their family and enjoy increased confidence and self-esteem. Parents, they say, should start early and enlist the help of their children as soon as they are able to hold their heads upright. Even infants, the experts argue, are able to absorb messy kitchen spills with their diapers and ingest the dust bunnies under the living room couch.

Apparently, I'm doing something wrong, because I have teenagers who can't identify the dishwasher, who still believe in the Garbage Fairy and who consider dust bunnies a protected species.

But maybe it's not too late for me to turn them into productive citizens with a strong sense of self-worth. Maybe it's time we put the labor back in Labor Day—for the sake of our children. Let's proclaim September 2nd National Chores Day. Nothing would make my long weekend sweeter than watching my kids sweat a little. Who knows, a day of work might not only build character, but also make going back to school seem like a pretty good idea.

Making Memories? Forget It

If you're thinking of taking a summer vacation with your young children, think again. You'll spend lots of time and money to create a week of magical moments in an exotic location. You'll provide them with educational experiences like whale watches and hands-on exhibits at children's museums. You'll arrange for once-in-a-lifetime opportunities such as swimming with dolphins or getting backstage passes to the Wiggles and guess what? They won't remember a thing.

I know, because just last night, I was watching television with my youngest son, Lewis, when a commercial for Disney World came on. Starry-eyed cherubs raced through the streets of the Magic Kingdom. Fireworks exploded over the Cinderella Castle and Mickey gleefully applauded.

"Remember when we were there?" I asked Lewis.

"No," he said. "I don't remember."

Now, our family has journeyed to Disney World twice. Granted, the first time we went, Lewis was *en utero*, so maybe, in all fairness, I can't expect him to remember that trip. But the second time we went, he was at least four or five. We spent three days tracking Mickey through the Magic Kingdom and when the big photo moment finally arrived, Lewis burst into tears and clung to my leg. How could he not remember?

I looked back at the commercial. The television tots embraced Mickey and the well-cast parents exchanged smug, self-congratulatory smiles that said "We're making memories that our kids will treasure for the rest of their lives." Hah!

In fact, it's been scientifically proven that kids have no, what researchers call, episodic memory until after age four. Four! That means everything that you do before then is essentially for nothing. You could travel to the Galapagos to pet the giant tortoises or stay home and watch the roller derby and drink beer and it wouldn't make a bit of difference. Your kids won't remember. That's because, according to scientists, the *corpus callosum*, the area of the brain which is critical in the formation of event memories, isn't fully developed until a child is four or maybe even five years old. My own personal research says it's not fully formed until they're at least twelve—maybe eighteen.

"Remember when you were six and we went to Niagara Falls and your brother threw up on the *Maid of the Mist*?" I asked.

"No," said Lew.

"How about when you were seven and we went to Washington, D.C., and our car got towed?"

"Nope."

"Or when we were camping in the Grand Canyon and the park ranger plucked you from the edge of the North Rim? You were eight. You've got to remember that."

"Nope," he said. "Well, I don't remember the canyon, but I sort of remember Dad yelling at me."

"He yelled so you wouldn't fall into the canyon," I pointed out.

"Well, I just remember the yelling," Lewis said.

Now, I was curious. "So," I probed. "What is your earliest memory?" I thought back on Lewis' twelve years and all the family vacations, the weekends at the lake, the August days at the shore, the Christmas mornings, the ice cream trucks and the birthday parties.

"I remember the time you forgot to pick up me from kindergarten and I had to wait for you in the principal's office for a really long time," Lewis said.

"C'mon, that's your earliest memory?" I prodded.

"I remember when it was my birthday at preschool and you didn't bring cupcakes." Sheesh.

Maybe it's not too late to book a trip to Disney and make some memories this summer.

8

Animal Husbandry

A Household Word: **Libido**

After I had my first baby, I went for my six-week checkup. "Have you resumed sexual relations?" the doctor inquired. SEX?! I hadn't even had a shower.

LEAVE IT TO DADDY

Since I left my full-time job and became a full-time mom, my husband has been a little envious of my stay-at-home status. He doesn't think that being in the house all day with three kids is all that tough. He maintains that if he were in charge of the home front, things would be different ... calmer, quieter, and neater, too.

He thinks that the minute he leaves for work I order pizza and invite the entire PTO over to watch the soaps and use his razors. He might even suspect that I devote a portion of each day to rubbing the cat on the furniture.

Or sneaking into his closet to cut the buttons off his sport coats and drip red wine on his ties.

Or stuffing empty juice boxes and overdue library books under the seats of the station wagon and systematically unfolding all the roadmaps.

Or driving around aimlessly until the car starts to make a strange noise or someone backs into it.

Or asking the kids to conduct experiments involving his shaving cream and the microwave.

Or turning on all the lights and appliances to see how fast the electrical meter can spin.

Or ripping the last five checks out of the checkbook—just for sport. Ha!

That was before I walked out.

I left my husband and three kids to go to my high school reunion. I would be gone one whole night. I was pretty sure that they would survive. I had posted the schedule of soccer, baseball and Cub Scout activities on the fridge. The cleats, shin pads and neckerchief were hanging by the front door and the pajamas and clothes for the next fourteen hours were laid on the kids' beds. There was food, a full tank of gas and there was 911. There was also a fifth of bourbon.

When I got to the hotel where my girlfriends and I were staying, my cell phone rang. Visions of ambulances, dismemberments and accidental poisonings flashed through my brain.

"Hello?"

"Carol," my husband sounded out of breath. Heart attack? I wondered. House fire? "Where's the Little League game?"

"At the field next to the school," I said.

"Okay," he panted. "Don't worry, we're fine."

And they were. When I got home the next day everyone was alive.

"Dad made pancakes for supper," Lewis reported.

Sure, there were dirty dishes were stacked in the sink, the kids looked like they were dressed by color-blind clowns, the downstairs toilet was backed up and the lights were on in every room. But there was a "welcome home" bouquet on the kitchen table and it looked like my husband had even made a special effort to rub the cat on the couch.

MISSION TRANSMISSION

Why is it that my husband, who claims he can't hear a child wailing in the middle of the night, in the very next room, is able to detect a tiny little sound coming from deep within a car engine? Maybe it has something to do with the way he can pick up the scores to college basketball games even when the sports announcer reads them really, really fast, but can't comprehend when I say very slowly and clearly "Not tonight."

"Can't you hear that noise?" he demands. We've just wolfed down a pizza, jumped into the minivan and are already late for the end-of-the-year parent-teacher conference at the middle school.

"You mean the bike helmets rolling around in the backseat?" I say wiping tomato sauce off my lips and applying a more flattering shade of gloss.

"No, that rattling noise," he says, as he presses on the accelerator.

"My teeth? My nerves?" I think, as we race for our ten-minute audience with our son's teacher.

"Could it be the cans for recycling in the trunk?" I venture, as I pull down the visor mirror to pick a bit of basil off my bicuspids.

"No, it's coming from the engine," he says, squinting at the tachometer.

My husband rarely drives our minivan. When he does get behind the wheel, he notices every little thing. "The front left tire looks low," he reports. "The rear window needs a new wiper blade.... How did the door get scratched?" All of these observations, from a guy who doesn't blink when I change my hair color.

"Listen ... hear it?" he asks.

I listen, I really do. But all I hear is my stomach rumbling. I think I ate too fast.

Although I spend about a third of my life in the minivan—dropping my kids off at play practice, guitar lessons, soccer scrimmages and their friends' houses or waiting to pick them up at play practice, guitar lessons, soccer scrimmages and their friends' houses—I spend very little time thinking about how the van works ... until it doesn't. I put the key into the ignition, press on the gas and it moves forward—that's all I expect. Between threatening eleven-year-old boys who throw Cheez-Its and wrestle instead of putting on their seat belts, waving off the advances of a dog who breathes in my ear like an obscene phone caller and dealing with my daughter who changes the radio station whenever I start to sing, I am frankly more concerned about bloodshed in the backseat than whether or not the motor is misfiring. With all the noise that's inside the car, I'm blissfully unaware of the fan belt slipping—although I can't say the same thing about my sanity. But tonight, on the road to the school, it's just the two of us. It's quiet and, dare I say … almost romantic.

"Do you have any gum?" I ask my husband, as he pulls into the school parking lot. "I've got garlic breath."

"You really can't hear that cha-chink it makes when I give it gas?" he says, ignoring my obvious advances.

"I'm not sure," I falter. "But I think *I've* got gas."

He turns and looks at me with a serious expression. "Well, let's get it looked at and taken care of as soon as possible."

"Oh, honey, I don't think that's really necessary. I'll be alright. It was just the pizza," I say, touched by his compassion.

"I was talking about the car," he replies.

"What about it?"

There's a noise coming from the engine!" he fumes.

"Really? I don't hear anything."

STICK TO YOUR GUNS

When our first child was born, my husband and I both agreed (at least I *thought* we both agreed) that we would not allow our son to play with toy guns. Guns, we asserted—even water pistols shaped like animals—promote violence, aggression and general boy-like behavior that I worried would lead my child to torture neighborhood cats and build explosives in our basement.

I protected my firstborn as best I could from anything remotely violent. I hid the front page of the newspaper to shield him from images of war. I refused to watch the nightly news—even after he went to bed—lest the word "kill" drift into his subconscious. I even boycotted our town's annual Fourth of July parade because the Revolutionary War re-enactors carried reproduction muskets that they fired with a fiendish delight all along the parade route.

I felt smug. I had done my job. My child was almost five and he had never heard the word "gun," or been exposed to anything more violent than a sneeze. He was pure and innocent and peace-loving ... or so I thought.

Then, one morning at breakfast, he waved a half-eaten slice of toast and made a sound with his mouth that exactly mimicked an Uzi submachine gun.

"Phhhhhhhhhhhtttttttttttttttt!"

"Is that a little airplane?" I asked anxiously.

"No, it's a shooter," he replied, calmly aiming the toast at me.

I was appalled. How had this happened? I thought back to my college psychology classes and theories of the collective unconscious.

"Do you want Mommy to put jelly on your toast?" I asked, hoping to squash his imagination.

"No toast, shooter," he insisted as he nibbled the crust to a greater realism. I was horrified, but my husband remained calm.

"Boys like to shoot stuff," he reasoned. "I spent my entire childhood playing with toy guns and I'm not a violent person."

This is true. My husband refuses to whip cream. He's a gentle soul who catches the mice that invade our kitchen in a "Havahart Trap," then chauffeurs them to more prestigious neighborhoods.

"Maybe by forbidding guns, you're making them seem more exciting," he suggested. Apparently, Harris had also taken Psych 101.

The next day my husband came home with a bag from Toys 'R' Us. "Whaddaja bring me? Whaddaja bring me?" Nathan said as he tore into the plastic packaging and released his prize—a shiny toy pistol with a brown plastic holster and a clip-on sheriff's badge. That's when I went ballistic.

"I thought we agreed to no guns!" Clearly, there was a link between toy guns and acts of real violence, because I wanted to kill my husband. "How could you buy this without checking with me first?"

"Cowboys don't count," my husband said. "Roy Rogers had guns, so did John Wayne—they're not psycho killers—they're American icons." My son buckled the holster around his waist and scampered outside making realistic ricochet sounds with his mouth.

"It's still a gun," I brooded, as I watched my child in the back yard taking aim at trees and imaginary outlaws. I hoped none of the neighbors were looking out their windows. "Other parents won't let him play with their kids anymore," I warned. "None of the other children are allowed to have toy guns. Everyone will think we're terrible parents."

But I was wrong. The cowboy pistol marked the end of our neighborhood arms accord and, in just a few days, every child was weighed down with weaponry. They were packing Nerf guns, strapping on super squirters and twirling Ninja Turtle nunchucks. Now, I tell myself that although my child is running around the block yelling "Hit the dirt!" he is also getting exercise, breathing fresh air and, best of all, he is out of the house. Fortunately, there have been no casualties, just the near collapse of my marriage and the realization that there are some battles that I just can't win.

OPPOSITES ATTRACT

My own unscientific research, conducted over two decades of domestic bliss, has proven that opposites not only attract, they get married. It seems like my most gregarious friends have husbands whom I suspect have taken vows of silence. The men who are gourmet cooks have wed skinny women who think that Outback Steakhouse is adventurous dining, and the happy-go-lucky types tend to end up with spouses whose worry extends to the dog's cholesterol level. Maybe it's nature's way of strengthening the gene pool.

My husband and I are opposites, too. He likes to make lists, I like to make mojitos. He always has his cell phone; mine is always in my other purse. He thinks I should make dinner; I think we should get Chinese take-out. While most of these little differences are almost endearing, there's one area that has caused actual friction in our otherwise near-perfect union: My husband is neat and I am, well … not.

After two decades, you might have thought that some of his fastidiousness would have rubbed off on me. But like cat hair on the couch, I cling to my slovenly ways. I've even tried to convince my spouse that the papers piled on top of my desk and clothes on the bottom of my closet are indicators of creativity and superior intellect and that my husband's neckties, hanging chromatically, are surely a sign of a deep-rooted neurosis.

Still, for me, this unequal yoking is a pretty good deal. My husband never leaves the toilet seat up, he does his own laundry and his socks are matched, rolled and arranged by fiber content in his drawer (okay, that's a little over the top). He even cleans the kitchen after dinner and, I have to say, he looks pretty hot in an apron. Sometimes, though, his drive to tidy makes me crazy—like when I park at a meter downtown and there's no loose change under the floor mats because he has just vacuumed the car or when I scribble an important phone number in the dust on the coffee table and he wipes it away with Pledge. It can be irritating.

Just yesterday, I came home from the grocery store, dropped the bags on the counter, put the milk into the fridge and stashed a box of popsicles in the freezer. "Stop!" said my husband as he swept into the kitchen. "I organized the cabinets for you."

"Okay," I said as I opened the cupboard and tossed in a bag of egg noodles.

"Wait!" he shrieked. "Don't put those there. I've arranged things so that you'll always be able to find them."

"I could find stuff before," I said trying to sound reasonable.

"Well, I couldn't," he sniffed. "The kids wanted lunch and I couldn't find the peanut butter, so I did a little reorganizing."

"Peanut butter is in the fridge," I said brightly. "It's organic."

"Well, now it's here," he opened a cabinet with a flourish to reveal shelves of precisely stacked cans and jars. "It's with the other stuff that comes after M"

"Huh?"

"Peanut butter," he explained as though he was talking to a very small child. "It starts with P. All food that begins with the letters A through M is on the left side of the stove. The N through Z stuff is on the right."

"So, where does the spaghetti go?" I inquired, "under N for noodles or I for Italian or …"

"P for pasta," he said pointing to neatly displayed boxes of linguini, no boil lasagna and Easy Mac.

He flashed a triumphant smile and went off to hunt dust bunnies and alphabetize his CDs. I opened each cabinet and marveled at the transformation. From anchovies to ziti the kitchen cabinets were a vision of orderliness. It was like Benetton—only with canned goods. It was so neat that it didn't even feel like my kitchen. So I unloaded the rest of the bags and put everything away, carefully filing it all under "F" for … well, food.

HAPPY UNMOTHER'S DAY

Mother, it's your special day! We hope it's special in every way!—Hallmark Greetings

"Honey, I called everywhere and can't get reservations for brunch on Mother's Day," my husband apologized.

Good thing, I thought glumly, because the last thing I want to do on Sunday is to spend the morning monitoring my kids in an all-you-can-eat buffet line. The very thought gives me heartburn. Nagging my children to use their forks, sit up straight and stop kicking the table is not how I envision my special day.

It's not that I don't love spending time with my husband and kids; it's just that my ideal meal wouldn't include pigs in a blanket and three kids on a maple-sugar high. I'd rather dine on yellowtail sushi at a table for one.

"I could cook a big breakfast and we could all have a nice, relaxing morning together," my spouse offered.

That's the problem with Mother's Day, I brooded. Everyone expects you to spend it in the blissful bosom of your family, surrounded by kids—just like every other day. I guess I don't really want to celebrate Mother's Day. I want to celebrate UnMother's Day. It's not that I don't adore being a wife and mother, I do. But frankly, I embrace the joys of motherhood 364 days of the year. I'd like one day for me. For twenty-four hours, I'd like to forget that there are three people who owe their very existence to my reproductive powers. For just one day, I'd like to toss aside the mantle of motherhood and reacquaint myself with the person I was before I had kids. The freer, thinner, younger woman who blithely thought, "Yeah, three kids seems like a good idea."

"We could go out for an early dinner," my husband suggested.

I don't want to eat at a family-friendly restaurant, I silently sulked. I don't want dinner out, or breakfast in bed, or flowers, or cards. In fact, I don't want to see my kids for the whole day. I want a Mother's Day that's all about me. Not about what will make my family feel like they have done their job as prescribed by the folks at Hallmark.

I want to hike in the woods and not worry about being back in time to drive the carpool or cook dinner. I want to ride a Harley, write a poem and sit in a movie theater from dawn to dark. I want to swim with the dolphins, soar with the eagles and dig in my garden without feeling like I should be helping with homework, matching socks or defrosting hamburger. Call me blasphemous, but on Mother's Day, I don't want to be a mom.

We can go out to eat next weekend.

THE "H" WORD

A new business opened just down the street from my house. It's called "Rent a Husband." No kidding. My husband says that they probably send a guy over to watch basketball and fall asleep on your couch. Nope. Turns out, you can call to have a man (presumably someone else's husband) come and do stuff, like clean out your gutters or fix your back stairs.

Frankly, if I was going to pay good money to rent a husband, I wouldn't waste him on household chores. I'd rent one who liked to dance and bring him to my nephew's bar mitzvah or lease a man who wouldn't grumble about spending Friday night seeing a romantic comedy instead of a movie with car chases and submarines.

But I already have a husband and even though I will have to wait until the next Hugh Grant movie comes out on video, and beg my husband to dance at the bar mitzvah, he's a good guy with a steady job. The job is especially attractive, because when something breaks in our house, my husband doesn't grab his toolbox, he reaches for his wallet.

It's true; my husband is talented in many areas. He can name the entire 1976 lineup of the Philadelphia Phillies and his grilled steak tips are perfection—but he isn't handy. Neither of us is. In fact, at our house, the word is practically a profanity. We call it the "H" word.

There are handy guys out there. I've seen them at Cub Scout meetings where their sons race Pinewood Derby cars that look like they were engineered by NASA. The sleek lines are testimony to the dad's professional wood shop and prowess with a lathe. Our son's car is slopped with poster paint and festooned with Pokémon stickers, but he made it all by himself. When the other kid's car wins first place, the kid gets the trophy, but it's the dad who deserves it—for being handy. When our son's car careens off the track, we tell ourselves that building character is more important than winning a race. Our son, whose character is still under construction, sulks in the backseat as we drive home.

Handy guys are like sled dogs in the snow; they leave their mark everywhere. They remember to put down the toilet seat, and then stand on it to install skylights in the bathroom. They watch the NCAA playoffs and during half time they wire their family room for surround sound. When their Internet connection is down, they know how to get it back up. Handy guys see a problem and they get their drill bits. My husband sees a problem and he gets an estimate. It's hard not to be a little envious.

In my neighbor's back yard, there's a tree house that my kids adore and that I covet. It's got more square footage than my entire first floor. The kitchen is nicer, too. That's because the dad who lives next door to us is ... handy.

But, unlike the chickenpox or crabgrass, being handy isn't contagious. You can't catch it from your neighbors. Instead, you have to endure watching them tackle one fabulous home improvement project after another. New front steps, a backyard patio, bunk beds, and a home theater. It's enough to make you dread the weekend.

"Dad, can you build a real batting cage in our back yard?" my son asks my cornered husband. "Joey's dad made one and it's awesome!"

"Errr ... I'm not sure that we have room for something like that," Harris stalls. "But if you grab your glove, we can have a game of catch."

You know, it would be easy to rent a husband to build a batting cage in the yard or hire a hubby to install granite counter tops in the tree house, but I don't think there's any place where you can rent a dad.

9

Nobody Gets Gifts on Columbus Day

A Household Word: **Illumination**

My kids leave a room and never turn out the lights, or shut off their computers, or click off the television. I guess you could say that we celebrate the Festival of Lights—all year.

CORNERING ST. NICK

Last week, I was momentarily possessed by the Ghost of Christmas Presents, so I relented and took my youngest son to see Santa at the mall.

"I know that *you* won't buy me PlayStation 3," said Lew, "so I'm going to ask Santa for it." His face was aglow with anticipation. "Do you think he can get me an iguana, too?"

We found St. Nick holding court in a garland-festooned gazebo decked with glitter and fake snow. There was a big crowd waiting to see him. Children squirmed, parents forged lifelong friendships and one family used a cell phone to call for pizza delivery in a line that reached from Baby Gap all the way to next Christmas.

This was a new experience for me. Neither of my other kids would ever agree to sit on Santa's lap. Maybe they were scared of his power, his fake beard or his breath. Not Lewis. He had a mission and a list that included action figures, computer games and an iguana. The only way he was going to get that kind of stuff was to talk with The Great One himself. So we waited.

"Can iguanas live in the North Pole?" Lewis asked as the line crept forward.

After two bathroom breaks (the woman behind us held our place) and a quick trip to Mrs. Field's Cookies, we were almost there. A photographer, in full elf regalia, collected five dollars from each parent who wanted to document the precious holiday moment with a framed instant photo. Lewis quickly reviewed his list and I dug crumpled bills out of my purse. It was our turn!

I gave my son an encouraging little shove toward Santa's throne. He didn't move. He dug his sneakers into the plastic snowflakes and instead of clambering up on the velveteen knee, turned to me and said: "Actually, I changed my mind. I don't really want to see him."

"C'mon," I urged. "You waited so long." I could feel the eyes of the other parents bearing down on me. I wasn't ready to forfeit our audience with Santa. So I seized the opportunity and plunked myself on his ample lap. "Santa," I said. "I've been a good mom all year—just ask my kids. I did the laundry, paid for piano lessons and took everyone to the dentist twice. I chaperoned a field trip to the fish hatchery, watched soccer games in the rain and went out to buy poster board at eleven o'clock at night. I've hosted birthday parties, bought new winter jackets, and still, they want more. Santa, I'm the one who bakes the cookies that you eat at my house on Christmas Eve and it's me who reminds the kids to leave carrots for the reindeer. So now, I'd like a little something from you."

"Make it quick," Santa said. "My legs are getting numb."

"OK," I hissed into his ear. "Here's the deal. You promise to load up your sleigh with toys that don't need twenty AA batteries or a doctorate in physics to assemble. Fill the stockings with yo-yos and Play-Do, not Game Boys and Play-Station 3, and throw in a couple of lumps of coal to keep my kids humble. Bring them gifts that inspire creativity and cooperation, but don't bring them everything on their lists. I know that there is value in the gift of disappointment and, someday, they will, too. Keep leaving Legos, and puzzles, books and board games for the family under the tree and this year I won't leave any broken cookies for you or limp carrots for your reindeer. Santa, help my children believe in you and the magic of the season and I promise that I will do my best to keep your spirit alive at our house all year long, and to continue to teach my kids that the true joy of the holiday is not what you get, but what you give."

As the elf moved in for the photo opportunity, Santa winked, gave a nod, and then gently pushed me off his knees.

"Oh, one more thing, big guy," I whispered. "No iguanas."

BATTERIES NOT INCLUDED

There must be a special store where my relatives go to buy really loud toys. Maybe they don't know how many decibels three children can produce—even without a battery-operated karaoke machine—or maybe they just hate me.

I picture them cackling with fiendish delight as they shop and plot the demise of my sanity. For my children though, the highlight of the holiday season is the day the UPS truck delivers their package. While my kids are delirious with anticipation, I already know what's inside the box. Along with something like a salad shooter for me and an electric ice scraper for my husband, there will be large, loud, battery-operated toys for the kids—toys that promise "realistic battle sounds," "easy assembly" and "fun for the whole family!"—toys that any parents with common sense, functioning eardrums and a spine would never buy.

Batteries will not be included nor will any receipts or marks identifying point of origin. We will not be able to return or exchange these gifts. We will own them and my children will demand that I remove the batteries from every flashlight and smoke detector in the house to make the toys work. Now!

Maybe I should worry that the relatives who sent these gifts are exhibiting passive aggressive behavior or maybe it's simply that they have been to my house and know that in order for any toy to make itself heard above the roar of our everyday life it has to pack as many decibels as a real grenade launcher or wail like a neglected infant until I develop post-traumatic stress syndrome and my milk lets down.

It wasn't always like this. For a few years, I was successful in sheltering my children, and my mental health, from the loud reality of battery-operated toys. I told them that the little door on the bottom of the Rescue Heroes Headquarters was a bank and that the tiny compartment on the back of Baby Miracle Moves was to hold Cheerios.

In a world without batteries, they were content to push their remote control cars quietly around the living room, to pretend that they were receiving messages on their walkie-talkies, and to tend to baby dolls which, instead of speaking Spanish or demanding fake cereal, just slept.

Sure, I felt a little guilty, but my motives were noble. I only wanted to preserve the innocence of my children and maintain some semblance of peace and quiet in my home. Call me naive, but I always imagined that my kids would spend their days weaving wildflowers through their hair and staging puppet shows with marionettes they made from acorns and twigs.

In pursuit of that ideal, I not only withheld the double A's, I told them that the only station on television was PBS, that rice cakes were cookies and that computer games would burn out their retinas. They believed me. And, although my children never actually made anything out of acorns, I did enjoy a brief period of feeling smug about my superior parenting skills.

Then it all fell apart. They met other kids, went to their houses and came home with tales of wonder. The cookies were sweeter and more delicious, the TVs got hundreds of stations and the toys could talk, sing and move. Melissa's Baby Miracle Moves cooed and giggled. Sam's Rescue Heroes had voice-card technology. When the friends came to play at our house, they politely nibbled the rice cakes and appraised our mute playthings.

"That's not a bank, you dope," their friends pointed out. "It's where the batteries go."

"Batteries?" A light went on that required no Duracells. My kids glared at me with looks of betrayal.

"Moooooooommmmmmmmm!!!"

The jig was up.

Turns out, battery-operated toys have one quality that is pretty appealing. They don't keep going and going and going. After a few days, the batteries die, the moving parts scatter far under the couch and the toys are silent. So before the box comes this year, I think I'll be prepared with extra AA batteries for the noise reduction headphones that I've requested from Santa.

Wii Wish You a Merry Christmas

It's 4:30am on a December morning. It is still dark outside and yet I am pulling sweatpants on over my pajamas, zipping up my parka and grabbing a travel mug for my coffee. What rouses me from a warm bed to greet the chilly dawn? The search for a Nintendo Wii.

Every year, my youngest son, Lewis, makes a Christmas list. It's an exercise in greed and it's a chance for him to cling to the possibility that there just might be a Santa. He usually asks the big guy for the stuff he knows I hate—stuff like toy guns, video games and battery-operated grenade launchers. Most years, Lewis' list has ten or fifteen items ranging from socks to an Enzo Ferrari. Last year, however, there was just one thing he wanted: a Nintendo Wii.

For those parents whose kids only play with educational toys, the Wii, pronounced "we," is an interactive, video-type game. Don't ask me to explain it any more except to say that kids play it standing up and there is a flailing of limbs involved so, theoretically, it almost qualifies as exercise. Almost. That was Lewis' argument as he explained that although the Wii was expensive, he wouldn't want anything else for Christmas or ever again—even if his brother and sister had lots of presents to open—and he only had a Nintendo Wii.

"We'll see," I said and began checking the flyers in the Sunday papers. But the Wii was not only sold out in every store, there were long waiting lists, inflated internet auctions and entire websites devoted to tracking rumored deliveries of the Wii system at stores in our area.

I paid ten dollars for a password and access to one of the prophetic websites and drove to the store that was listed as having the coveted Wii. "Sorry," the kid at Best Buy said. "We had a few, but you have to get here before the store opens. People line up at five o'clock in the morning."

He was right. The next Saturday, when I pulled into the store parking lot at 4:45am, there was already clutch of would-be Wii owners on the sidewalk. There were mothers from neighboring towns relaying information on their cell phones, indulgent grandparents who had made promises to grandkids and computer geeks who simply wanted to own the latest toy. And there was me. Was I like these folks who obviously had no lives; who obviously had forgotten the true meaning of Christmas? The answer obviously, was yes (*oui*, Wii!)

They say that people who share intense life experiences develop deep and lasting bonds. This is how I felt about my new friends as we waited outside the store in the frosty darkness. We stamped our feet to keep warm, talked about our families and swapped stories of the Wiis that got away. We shared coffee and rumors of deliveries and collective disappointment when the store manager stuck his head out of the front entrance and said "Sorry, no Wiis today."

For several Saturdays, I made the pre-dawn pilgrimage to the parking lots of Target, Best Buy, Costco and Wal-Mart. The faces of the desperate parents, grandparents and geeks were different each week, but the story was always the same. No Nintendo Wii.

I'd like to say that on Christmas morning, like in the song where the scarlet ribbons miraculously appear in gay profusion on the little girl's bed, or the Jean Shepherd movie where the kid finally gets a BB gun, that a Nintendo Wii somehow appeared under our tree. But it didn't. Instead, Lewis got Legos, a cool clock radio, a bathrobe and the gift of disappointment which, I believe builds character, but doesn't produce joyous squeals of delight on Christmas morning. Somehow though, he survived the season and muddled through the year.

Then, just a few weeks ago, I walked into my neighborhood video store and lo and behold—there was a stack of sleek white boxes.

"Are those Wiis?" I asked the teenage clerk."

Yep," he said, "just got 'em in."

"I'll take one!" I said and shelled out what seemed like a lot of money for a box that seemed somehow too small to deliver a big impact on Christmas morning.

This year there will be shouts of delight, Kodak moments and a renewed belief in the power of Santa. This year I won't have to stand in line with the lunatic fringe of the consumer culture. This year there will be interactive video fun for the whole family and I will be *The Mom Who Saved Christmas!* I hid the Wii under my bed and reveled that my Christmas shopping was basically done … until Lewis handed me his wish list. There was only one item on it … an Xbox 360 "It's way more fun than the Wii," Lewis said. "If I get one, I won't ever want anything else."

Like the song says, it really is the most wonderful time of the year … to give, to receive and to save your receipts.

LOVE CHILD

It's February and any day now my son will come home from school with a list of his classmates' names. The list is for Valentine's Day. There are twenty-three kids in Lewis' fourth-grade class and he will need to have a card for each child—even the girls.

When I was a kid, how many valentines you got was an accurate reflection of how popular you were. It wasn't a holiday for wimps and it wasn't politically correct. Now, every kid sends a card to every other kid. The girls also send cards to the teacher, the student teacher, the crossing guard, the school bus driver, the school nurse, the principal and the lunch ladies.

I have no problem with the sentiment. The problem is that my son would rather do anything—take a bath, eat creamed spinach, even clean his room—before he would put a pen to paper. Especially to send valentines. Especially to girls, who are gross.

So writing out the cards becomes a struggle—me nagging and pleading, him postponing and making excuses. It could take weeks to write out twenty-three valentines for the children in his class (never mind the ones for the principal and the nurse). It almost makes homeschooling seem appealing. Almost. Maybe I should look into military academy. I bet the cadets don't have to send valentines to their sergeants.

I know that there's probably an upside to having to write out nearly two dozen cards. For one thing, it will give him fodder for future psychotherapy sessions. He'll also get a chance to practice his cursive and maybe develop his math skills: "If there are twenty-four valentines in a box and Lewis messes up sixteen envelopes, how many envelopes will his mother have to make out of notebook paper?"

When my son was in preschool, it was different. I bought doilies and construction paper so that we could spend an afternoon together making cards for his ten little classmates. While Lewis peeled dried glue off of his fingers and cut paper hearts that looked like spleens, I copied his clumsy signature and signed every card "Love, Lewis." Now, he never signs his valentines "with love."

"Love is mushy, love is gross, love is for girls," he grumbles.

Now, he demands macho valentines that feature superheroes or military motifs. Last year, we compromised on Harry Potter valentines—but I had to buy two extra boxes because Lewis wouldn't use the cards with pictures of Hermione. This year, I know that even if we find cards with pictures of Patriot's quarterback Tom Brady or a portrait of Chuck Norris, that after writing his name on four or five cards, the signature will degenerate from a labored but legible "Lewis Band" to a hastily scrawled "Lew."

What if I had named him Zbigeniew?

After six or seven cards, he'll start to complain that his fingers are cramping, that he's starving, that he's exhausted and that he feels like he is going to throw up. Before he's gotten through half the names on the list (forget the cards for the lunch ladies), he'll abandon the project entirely.

This year, I'm not going to turn Valentine's Day into a battle. I won't threaten or nag him to do all of his valentines. I'll just gather the cards that he didn't finish and neatly forge his name. I'll send cards to the teacher, the crossing guard and the bus driver, too. And I'll sign every valentine "With love."

Even the ones to the girls.

MOTHER'S DAY ROCKS

Every Mother's Day I get a rock. I'm not talking about the kind that's weighed in carats or set in sterling silver. I'm talking about the ordinary, igneous or sedimentary garden-variety rock. Oh sure, sometimes they are painted green or disguised as paper weights. Sometimes they have googly eyes or are covered with glitter, but I'm not fooled. I still can tell it's a rock.

A recent survey concluded that what women really want for Mother's Day is jewelry. Duh. The same highly scientific survey also discovered that what we don't want is anything related to housework. Double duh. Last year, my husband gave me a Swiffer. I wore it on a chain around my neck. I don't think he got the hint. He's the kind of guy who says "You're not my mother," and leaves the Mother's Day gift ideas up to the kids. That's why I get rocks.

Of course, the first time your preschooler hands you a lump of decorated granite and lisps "Happy Muvver's Day," it's pretty sweet. I know I got all misty and Hallmark-mommyish when my son gave me my first rock, err … I mean "paperweight." It was apparent that he had worked hard gluing and painting at the Sunshine Nursery School.

"This is beautiful!" I exclaimed. "I'll put it on my desk and keep it forever. How did you know this is exactly what I wanted for Mother's Day? You painted it all by yourself? You glued the little plastic eyes and sprinkled on all the glitter? I love it!"

I guess I was pretty convincing, because the next year I got another rock, only this one didn't have googly eyes or glitter.

"This is great! I don't have a blue one. I could really use another paperweight!"

When he was in kindergarten, I got another rock. And one the next year … and another one the year after that. It became apparent that his artistic efforts were beginning to erode.

"This is the prettiest rock I've ever seen. I'm glad that you didn't paint it or anything because it has such nice natural colors." And another one the next year.

"Wow! This rock is huge. I bet if I brushed the dirt off, it would make a great doorstop."

This year, as I lay in bed on Mother's Day morn, my husband brought me a cup of coffee and my son, Lewis, balanced a plate of toast on the nightstand.

"Happy Mother's Day," he announced without even the trace of a lisp.

"Thank you, sweetie," I said and took a charred bite.

He handed me a beautifully wrapped package. "What a nice job you did on the wrapping," I said as I ripped open the paper. My boy was growing up. This was an actual gift. Lewis had had made a jewelry box, painted it and decorated it with colored beads. It was lovely, in a gaudy, sort of more is more, kind of way. "Open it up, Mom" Lewis said.

I did, and there was a rock.

PRESTO CHANGE-OH!

My youngest son, Lewis starts talking about what he wants to be for Halloween in April.

Last year it went something like this: In May, he wanted to be a blood-sucking zombie. In June, he was set on Stone Cold Steve Austin, and in July he was sure that he wanted to be a ninja warrior. Although I tried to steer him toward costumes that wouldn't incite my neighbors to report me to the authorities, Lewis has faith that every October I will be able to help him morph into whatever disgustingly morbid or macabre creature he fancies—and he might be right. I have created ghosts out of almost new, one-hundred percent cotton bed sheets, dismantled my dining room and set up the sewing machine, put scissors to cloth to create a convincing mummy, and used up countless rolls of heavy duty aluminum foil to wrap robots, clad knights in shining armor and sheath the Tin Man.

But I'm not complaining. I see Halloween as an opportunity to prove that my year as an art major wasn't a total waste. And I challenge any abstract expressionist to make a Little Mermaid costume that can be worn over a late-fall jacket.

By last August, Lewis had abandoned the ninja idea. He wanted to be a wizard. Sure, I knew that he'd probably change his mind a hundred times before Halloween. Still, I was pleased. A wizard costume sends a good message to the neighbors. Wizards are rooted in literature. There's Merlin, Gandolf and Harry Potter. If my son roams the neighborhood in a wizard costume, I reasoned, people might think that we're well-read, well-bred and possibly even British.

The costume itself would be testimony to my competence as a mother. A child who wears a wizard costume is unquestionably the product of a home that's brimming with creative energy, good books and a mom who knows her way around a glue gun. A kid who's a ninja has a mom who lets him watch too much TV. A kid who's a ninja has a mom whose creativity is limited to dragging her kid's black sweatpants out of the dirty laundry basket.

"Are you sure you still want to be a wizard?" I asked Lewis during the last week of September.

"Yes," he said.

"You wouldn't rather be a ghost?" I probed. "We've got the sheets."

"I really want to be a wizard," he said.

"Yesssss!" I silently cheered, and mentally made a note of the things I would need for the costume: a light-up wand, purple satin, glitter, a pointy hat and spirit gum to stick on a fake gray beard. Still, there was plenty of time for him to change his mind.

By mid-October, Lewis hadn't wavered from his costume decision, so I bought two yards of purple satin. The silky material bunched up when I tried to cut it and slid onto the floor when I tried to sew a straight hem. I broke two needles on my sewing machine and used some scary language.

"You'd make a great ghost," I said to Lewis, after the bobbin jammed for the fourth time. "I want to be a wizard," he replied with conviction.

So I became consumed with making the costume and hand-sewed twelve silver stars onto the satin cloak. It was a lot of work, but when I jabbed my fingers with the needle, the shiny purple fabric hardly showed the bloodstains. We had pizza delivered three nights in a row. At five o'clock in the evening on October 30th, I finished making Lewis' wizard hat, called in an order of pork lo mein and summoned my son into the dining room to try on the finished product. The cloak fit perfectly and the silver stars sparkled. Lewis scrutinized himself in the mirror and when I placed the pointed purple wizard hat on his head he said, "I look like a dork. I want to be a ninja."

"But you said that you wanted to be a wizard. I spent three weeks slaving over this costume," I tried to reason with him.

"I changed my mind," he said. "Now I hate wizards. I want to be a ninja. He pulled off the purple cloak and the pointed hat and stood there in his black sweatpants and turtleneck. "This can be my costume," he said.

"We'll have to put reflective tape all over it so cars won't hit you," I cautioned.

"I don't care," he said. "I want to be a ninja." He tied a scrap of the purple satin around his head and began karate-chopping the air, ninja-style. The next night, I took Lew and three of his friends (all dressed in black sweatpants) trick-or-treating around the neighborhood. The reflective tape shone against the back of his black turtleneck and down the length of his sweatpants. It didn't bother him that some people mistook him and his friends for the California Raisins. "I'm a ninja," he explained over and over again. I followed behind him, holding the wizard costume, just in case he changed his mind.

10

Homeward Bound and Gagged

A Household Word: **Rich**

My neighbor Mimi has the right attitude. After seeing a documentary on Picasso, she noted that the house where he grew up was crammed with books and paints and paper—frankly it was a mess. Yet the narrator stated that the artist had been nurtured in a "rich environment." That sounds much better than saying that there is a fungus growing in the fridge and that piles of back issues of National Geographic are blocking the back door.

RED WHITE AND BEIGE

Okay, I admit it. I am hooked on HGTV. That's House and Garden Television for those of you who watch only *Masterpiece Theatre* and don't have cable. Shows like *Decorating on a Dime. Add Color!* and *Divine Design* are my guilty pleasure. Watching a team of experts come into a house and, in a tidy half-hour episode, transform a hovel like mine into a house that looks like nobody lives there—well, that's my idea of entertainment.

Of course I don't want my house to look like nobody lives here; I just want it to look like *we* don't live here. Heck, I'd even settle for having one room that doesn't look like it was decorated by Fisher-Price and a pair of wild raccoons. With that vision, I decided to redo our dining room.

On television, the decorators usually start the transformation by painting the walls a warm, rich color. Paint, they say, is the fastest way to change the look of a room—but then, they've never met my kids. In just a few short years, our walls have acquired a grimy patina of dirty hand prints, greasy fingerprints and a few inexplicable footprints near the ceiling. Underneath, is a meek shade called "White Coffee." Okay, it's beige. My whole house is beige. Beige is safe. Beige is neutral. Beige goes with everything, even greasy fingerprints and wild raccoons.

But, inspired by HGTV and armed with confidence, courtesy of the Home Depot ("You can do it, we can help") commercials, I was determined to break out of my flesh-toned rut and into the realm of color. So, on Saturday morning, when my husband went on his weekly pilgrimage to the hardware store, I went too, in search of the perfect pigment.

While Harris fondled cordless drills, I looked at paint chips. In the rainbow display at the back of the store I was immediately drawn to "Safari," "Barley," "Golden Retriever," "Clove Dust" and "Toast." That's because they are all beige.

That's when I realized that I am seduced by the romantic names on each color chip and I would never have painted my walls "White Coffee" if that same shade had been called "Band-Aid" or "Indecision."

I worked my way through the rack of chips from yellows—"Lemon Chiffon," "Saffron," "Paella" and "Squash"—to the greens—"Sweet Pea," "Key Lime" and "Asparagus." My stomach rumbled and I moved onto the reds.

Last year, red was touted as the new neutral and everybody in my town seized the moment by painting their dining rooms "Sangria" and "Raspberry Truffle." Everybody but me. Now, I wondered, was it too late? Will "Watermelon" walls scream 2006? I compared "Tomatillo" with "Enchilada," "Chili" with "Hot

Tamale." I craved a burrito. Maybe red really does stimulate the appetite. Maybe I shouldn't paint the dining room until after I lose ten pounds.

This year, the folks at HGTV say that orange is the new red. So I stuffed "Cancun," "Mai Tai" and "Tequila Sunrise" into my purse along with "Claret" and "Cherry Wine." It was nine-thirty o'clock in the morning, why did I want a drink?

At home, I fanned out the paint chips like I was holding a royal flush on *Celebrity Poker.* "What color should we paint the dining room?" I asked my kids.

"Light purple," said my daughter.

"Silver," said the youngest, pointing to my wedding band.

"That's gold, you moron and it's not even a color," his sister explained tenderly.

"Is too!"

"Is not!"

"Paint it black," my teenage son suggested, unwittingly quoting The Rolling Stones.

"What's wrong with the color it already is?" my husband asked.

"Well, nothing, really," I said "But HGTV says that warmer, richer colors can actually increase the appetite, stimulate conversation and encourage guests to linger."

"Those don't necessarily sound like good things," he replied, as I tacked the chips to the walls.

Over the next few days, I consulted with the neighbors, conferred with friends and solicited the opinion of the mailman, the paper boy and the pizza delivery guy.

"Definitely red," said the guy from Domino's, pointing to a square called "Pepperoni."

"Maybe light blue or green," said my neighbor Denise, giving a nod to "Sea Foam" and "Sea Glass." "Anything but red."

I carried chips everywhere I went. I asked the opinion of the supermarket cashier, my gynecologist and the vet. I examined the chips in sunlight, under fluorescent bulbs and by candlelight. I held them up to the woodwork, the furniture, the drapes and the dog.

Then I went to the hardware store and bought a roller, a drop cloth and a gallon of scrubbable latex paint. I'm finally ready to show my true color, and it's beige ... err, I mean "White Coffee."

The Grass is Always Greener

Like many urban hipsters, when we had our first baby, my husband and I decided that our child needed certain things that city life simply couldn't provide—things like a school system that would foster his obvious giftedness and a yard where he could safely frolic and sample fistfuls of dirt. So we moved out of our one-bedroom apartment and into a four-bedroom Victorian with a tiny yard, in a town that we hoped would combine easy access to the city with all the advantages of suburban life.

Turns out, that suburban life, even in neighborhoods with tiny yards, involves lawn care. It also turns out that while I have absolutely no interest or experience in this area, Harris has even less. Consequently, the "lawn" has become my turf. For years, I've rationalized the profusion of weeds by saying that only boring suburbanites agonize over crabgrass; that plush, green lawns aren't politically correct. And, although I knew that Al Gore would approve of my organic weeds, I knew my neighbors did not.

Oh, they didn't come right out and say "Your lawn sucks," they disguised their disgust by offering up neighborly advice. "Crabgrass means you're not watering enough," said the woman whose velvety back yard abuts mine. "At least it's green, "I'd reply. "My brother in law has a landscaping business," the neighbor across the street hinted. "Here's his card."

Frankly, the pressure was getting to me. So, last Saturday, I ripped up what I once considered to be perfectly good, crabgrass in the quest for lawn perfection.

What I found was grubs—lots of grubs. In fact, my yard had enough writhing larvae to keep Fear Factor on the air indefinitely. Why does my soil look like it was smote by a Biblical plague, while my neighbors' lawns are green and pest-free? According to the guy at the hardware store, the answer is chemicals. Of course, when my kids were little and regularly ingesting significant amounts of yard, using any type of pesticide would have been out of the question. But, now that they are older and stay indoors, safely basking in the glow of the Xbox-360, perhaps a little diazinon wouldn't hurt.

At the hardware store I bought *Grub-B-Gone* which promised to not only eliminate grubs, but also to kill waterfowl, cause permanent blindness and etch concrete. I can't speak for the grubs, but I was terrified.

Fortunately, before dead ducks dropped from the sky, my next door neighbor intervened. "Have you tested your soil? You might just need nitrogen or phosphate or potash," she said as she scooped up some of my grubby dirt, sealed it in a zip lock bag and headed back to her house. "I'll get back to you in a few minutes." Frankly, I was calmer waiting for the results of my EPT. A few minutes later, she was back, triumphantly waving a vile of light blue water. "Guess what," she beamed. "It's a boy?" I ventured. "No," she said "you need nitrogen." Indeed, according to the color chart on the home soil test kit, my dirt was malnourished, vitamin deprived and sickly. Who knew lawns need to eat? I felt like a bad parent.

She brought over a bag of organic fertilizer with nitrogen and sprinkled it around my yard like the lawn fairy. Together we tossed on the grass seed and watered it with the hose. Then we sat down on the porch, had a beer and waited for the grass to sprout. Sure, it takes a village to raise a child, but it takes a neighborhood to grow a lawn.

GROSS-ERY SHOPPING

I just went grocery shopping and spent $324.17, but there's still nothing for dinner. That's because I am a member of one of those wholesale clubs—a mammoth warehouse that sells everything from cashmere sweaters to sides of beef. It's not *really* a club—anyone who pays the annual forty dollar fee can shop there. If it was an *actual* club, they'd have a lounge with leather couches and a full bar for the high rollers like me. But maybe they think it's enough of a privilege to be able to buy tampons by the kilo.

The idea behind these places is that you save money because the club is "no frills." That means that there are no ceilings or shelves or clerks to unpack the crate of 8-oz. paper cups you need for the fourth-grade class party. Late at night, tractor trailers unload cubits of Pop-Tarts and twenty-gallon drums of ketchup directly into the warehouse, where incredible savings occur each time a club member walks down an aisle and thinks: "Yes, I *do* need five-gallons of pickle spears!"

I'm not sure if I'm saving money by shopping at this place, because calculating the price per unit requires math. But, there's an illusion of thrift because the experience is so unpleasant. The lighting is bad, there are piles of snow tires right next to the bakery section and everything is sold by the gross, so it must be cheap.

Warehouse stores aren't for everyone. You really have to be an optimist to shop here. When you invest in fifty pounds of dry dog food, you've got to believe that your pet is going to live long enough to eat it.

And there's some risk in buying bulk: When my youngest child was a toddler, I stocked up on disposable diapers. The kid turned out to be a potty genius and ten years later, I'm still using those Pampers to mop up spilled juice, dust furniture and wrap birthday gifts. At this rate, they'll last until my incontinent, golden years. What a bargain!

Grocery shopping with kids is never a good idea, and these behemoth stores are really no place for a youngster. They could easily get lost, be crushed by a case of Fruit by the Foot or accidentally wander into the furniture aisle and convince you to spend $500 on new bunk beds. But my kids love shopping at the food club. They enjoy the free samples and so do I. I figure that if we eat enough, we can mitigate the annual membership fee. The truth is, without the bits of kielbasa skewered on toothpicks, the tiny paper cups of canned fruit salad and bite-sized squares of microwaveable cheese Danish, club members wouldn't have the strength to push the oversized carts or lift sixty-four-packs of Go-Gurts from the shelf. Besides, free samples always taste better than food at home.

Lewis, the pickiest eater at home, will wolf down anything from strangers in the store.

"Mom, can you buy these?" he pleads through a mouthful of cheese ravioli. "I'll eat 'em every night."

"You'd have to eat them all tonight," I say. "There are 500 raviolis in each box, and we can't fit them into our freezer."

When I leave the store, a bouncer-type guy checks my photo ID and examines my register tape. It makes me want to defend my purchases. I want to tell him that I'm donating the gross of disposable razors to needy orphans, that I'm sending the kilo of Cracker Jacks to the troops in Iraq and that the twenty-pounds of kibble will provide holiday meals to puppies at the animal shelter. But I'm not. I'm just spending $324.17 on stuff for my family and, on the way home, I'll still have to stop at the grocery store and buy something for dinner.

FARM LIFE

My son Lewis, is at the kitchen table eating, Froot Loops and reading the back of the milk carton. It's organic milk, the carton explains, produced by cows whose blissful days on the farm are described like a spa vacation.

"Why can't *we* live on a farm?" Lewis asks with a newfound interest in the agrarian life.

"It's not all grazing in the grass and chewing your cud," I say. "For people, farms are hard work. There are lots of chores to do on a farm."

"I know, but it would be fun," he counters. "I could feed the chickens."

This from a kid whose goldfish, in a desperate act of self-preservation, jumped out of the bowl and tried to flop its way to the kitchen for a meal. This from a kid who promised, swore and crossed his heart that he would feed, walk and scoop the poop of a dog if we could pleeeeeeease just get one. Thinking that a dog would help teach responsibility, we went to the pound and adopted a shaggy mongrel. Now, the dog is slavishly devoted to me because, you guessed it, I feed him, I walk him and I scoop his poop. I remind Lewis of his promises regarding dog maintenance.

"But on a farm the chores would be more interesting," Lewis points out. "I could pick crops and stuff when they were ripe."

"Why don't you pick up your dirty soccer socks and put them in the washing machine?" I suggest. "They're ripe."

"The washing machine?" he looks confused. "Is that the white thing in the basement?"

Sigh.

If I had the chance to raise my kids all over again, with the wealth of knowledge that I have gleaned in two decades of parenting, I would do things differently. I would have sprung for the expensive wooden Brio train set as soon as my EPT turned pink, instead of waiting until my third child was three. I would have used the baby book I got as a shower gift to immediately record when each child took a first step or uttered "dada" because now, when say "Tell me about when I was little," I have to make stuff up and I would have resisted the pleas for hamsters, hermit crabs, geckos and goldfish. Right now, my freezer holds a Zip lock bag with the frozen carcass of a small rodent who, while awaiting a proper burial, is in real danger being misidentified as a pork chop. But mostly, if I could do it all again, I would make my kids do more chores.

It's not like I didn't try. We've had job charts and task wheels and incentive programs involving stickers, prizes and threats. I've offered money and taken away privileges. But my kids are a wily bunch.

"Nathan, can you bring in the trash cans?" I ask my oldest son after the garbage truck rumbles by in the morning.

"In a minute," he replies without looking up from the comics.

An hour later, I remind him that the empty cans are still on the curb.

"I'll get them as soon as I figure out my ride to the concert," he says as he taps instant messages into his laptop.

Before you can say "The Flaming Lips," he is rocking in the first row and the trash cans are rolling in the middle of our suburban street. I must have done something terribly wrong.

Other moms brag that their four-year olds clean the kitchen every night after dinner and make their own beds. I hear tales of toddlers, who wash and fold all of the family laundry, cook gourmet meals and scrub the bathroom grout with their toothbrushes. My three hardly lift a finger, and when they do, they want money.

"Will you give me twenty dollars to walk the dog?" Lewis asks.

"Not unless you walk him to Vegas and win," I say.

"If we lived on a farm," says Lew, "we wouldn't have to walk the dog. We could just let him out and he would herd the sheep and cows into the barn."

Lewis has a point. Maybe if I let the dog out, he will herd the empty garbage cans into the garage.

I CAN WAIT

I am in the dentist's waiting room. By some miracle of time and space, perhaps a worm hole at the end of my street, I have left the chaos of my kitchen and arrived five minutes early for my appointment.

I check in with the receptionist, sit down and pick a magazine to read while I wait. There is the *Journal of Periodontology* and a year-old copy of *Family Circle*. Naturally, I choose the *Family Circle*. By the time the receptionist calls my name, I have learned to make a holiday table runner, discovered the seven secrets to a successful marriage, and copied a recipe for pineapple upside-down cake. I am thoroughly enjoying myself.

"Dr. Yankowitz is running a little late," the receptionist warns. "I hope you don't mind waiting a few minutes."

Do I mind!? Is she kidding? I am thrilled! I am in a quiet room with comfortable chairs, reading material and no kids. This is the best part of my day—maybe even the best part of my summer.

When I left the house a few minutes ago, I put my two oldest children in charge of their younger brother. I handed them a box of Eggos, pointed them toward the toaster and told them that I'd be home in less than an hour. They could call my cell phone but only if there was a REAL EMERGENCY. "That's okay," I said to the receptionist. "I don't mind waiting. I don't mind a bit."

I finish the *Family Circle* and open the *Journal of Periodontology*. I am deeply engrossed in an article on dental implants when I hear the electronic strains of *The 1812 Overture*. After a few bars, I realize that it's not the office Muzak, it's my cell phone.

"Hi, Mom?" It's my youngest son, Lewis. He's shouting into the receiver and I think I hear sirens in the background.

"Honey, are you okay?"

"Uhmmm, can I have a popsicle?"

"Sure," I say and he hangs up before I can ask about the sirens. It's probably just the television.

I return to the *Journal of Periodontology* and read about gum disease and tissue inflammation. There are photos. I am having fun.

"Sorry to keep you waiting," the receptionist says. "I'm sure that Dr. Yankowitz will be right with you."

"It's fine," I say. "Really."

Now some people complain about waiting. Not me. I like it. Waiting is doing nothing, and I like doing nothing. In fact, I'm good at it. While I wait for my son at swimming lessons, I nap. While I'm on hold with the credit card company, I doodle. I even let people cut in front of me in the supermarket checkout line just so I can read celebrity gossip in the tabloids.

I'm never in a rush to get home because I know that although the house will probably still be standing, nobody will have let the dog out, closed a cabinet door, turned off a light, taken a coherent phone message or cleaned up anything that they spilled. I will have to referee fights, find lost sneakers, mop up dog pee and sponge melted popsicles from the upholstery. So, I don't mind waiting.

Beep beep beep beep BEEEEEP. It's Tchaikovsky again.

"Mom?" This time it's my daughter, Perry. "Lewisiseatingpopsiclesinthelivin-groomandit'smakingahugemessandhe'shoggingthettelevisionandit's ... NOT FAIR!" She pauses to catch her breath. "Also, when are you coming back, because I told Lindsay and Mia that you could drive us to the pool."

"I won't be long," I say. "But right now I'm waiting."

I hang up the phone, stroll down the hallway and take a sip from the water fountain. I use the restroom, examine my mouth for signs of gum disease and savor the experience of being uninterrupted.

Beep beep beep BEEEEEEEEEEP ...

"Mom?" It's my oldest son, Nathan. "Uh, I was making Eggos and there was a tiny mishap with the toaster. I think it's mostly smoke damage. The firemen said it was safe to go back in the house. Maybe you should write to the waffle company and ask for your money back."

I walk back to the waiting room, sit down and turn off the cell phone.

"Oh, Mrs. Band," the receptionist calls out. "We thought you had left. Dr. Yankowitz is seeing his 9:30 patient now. Would you like to make an appointment for another day?"

"No, thanks," I say. "I think I'll just wait."

FAMILY LIFE EXPOSED

I just picked up photos from our end-of-the summer family vacation and, as I studied them, I thought, "Gee, that really was the best vacation we ever had. It was perfect." Then, I came to my senses and remembered that although it was a good trip, there were plenty of moments that weren't documented on that roll of four by six inch, double prints.

In one photo, taken by a willing passerby, the five of us are standing on a beach smiling into the sun. Although you may see that image on our holiday card in December, what the photo doesn't reveal is that the kids had been bickering in the backseat of the car the whole way to the beach. My husband was tense because by the time got there, the parking lot was full and we had to pay twenty dollars to park in a swamp. Smile!

Another vacation photo depicts Lewis digging into a serious scoop of black raspberry ice cream. In a few years, we won't remember that after the picture was taken, he blew lunch all over the rental van. We won't remember because we don't have a picture of it. A quick check into the fifteen years of photos jammed into the shoe boxes in our basement reveals that my fond memories of the past may indeed be a result of failing to accurately document the bad and the ugly along with the good and the scenic. From our family photos, it would be easy to conclude that we live on a beach where it is always Christmas. This gross misrepresentation is an injustice to our future generations and to us. You need to remember the bad times in order to appreciate the good. Besides, in a few years the bad photos might be good for a few laughs ... or for blackmail.

My daughter's three-month bout of colic, the Thanksgiving Day when the garbage disposal backed up, my shag haircut, the time the car broke down in the tunnel downtown—these are just some of the moments I wish I had captured on film.

From now on, in the interest of historical accuracy and in the spirit of those popular reality-based television shows, I propose that families pay equal attention to getting snapshots of all aspects of daily life. Take pictures of your kids when they sit glassy-eyed playing Nintendo; get a close up of the idiot who cut you off at the intersection; and take a moment to snap a photo during the next spat with your spouse. "Honey, say 'cheese!" ... it's our first fight!"

Now, every moment can be a Kodak moment and, if you do an admirable job of honestly chronicling family life, your friends will probably beg to see the photos of your conference with the school principal or the pictures from the day that your cleaning lady didn't show up.

The next time the toilet overflows, the cat coughs up a hairball or one of the kids has a full-blown tantrum in the middle of the supermarket, I'll be sure to grab a camera and say "Okay, everybody ... Smile!" Click.

CALL ME MRS. BAND

Call me Mrs. Band. That's what I am going to tell kids when they come to my house. From now on the moniker of my mother-in-law will be my name, too. I've been intimidated by Mrs. Band for twenty years, so I'm betting that her handle will have the same effect on my kids' friends.

Because it galls me when a kid comes into the kitchen, opens the fridge and says. "Hey, Carol, got anything good in here?" I'm appalled when I drive kids home and they get out of the car and say "Bye, Carol," and slam the door without a word of thanks. Maybe everything went to heck when we started letting children call grown-ups by their first names. That simple innovation, begun back in the 1960's when everyone wanted to bridge the generation gap and be their kids' pals, has opened a floodgate of familiarity which, at my house, has bred contempt. My contempt.

Don't get me wrong. I want my kids to have friends; I want them to feel free to bring them home and I want to provide an atmosphere where they feel comfortable. Only lately, it seems that some of them have been feeling a little too comfortable, a little too entitled to my chauffeur services and whatever is in the pantry. Just yesterday, as I was making out my shopping list, one of Lewis' friends said, "Buy Fruity Pebbles, okay, Carol?"

I need to get control, demand respect and muster up some healthy intimidation and I think that Mrs. Band is the right gal for the job. I'm hoping that if kids think of me as Mrs. Band, they won't complain about what pizza joint I order from. I'm thinking that in Mrs. Band's house they will wait until they have been asked before downing the last of the orange juice. When they get a ride home in Mrs. Band's car, I'm almost certain that they'll remember to say "Thanks for the ride, Mrs. Band." At Mrs. Band's house, when she says it's time to go, they will promptly put on their shoes and head for the door. Ignoring her and continuing to play Guitar Hero or saying "Hang on, Carol," are not responses that Mrs. Band would tolerate.

It's even possible that the behavior of my own children could be positively influenced by the presence of Mrs. Band. Seeing your friends treat your mother with the utmost respect might make courtesy seem cool. I can almost envision my children clearing the dinner dishes, thanking me for the delicious dinner and cheerfully scampering off to bed. Almost.

Call me old-fashioned, but I think that titles, like Mr. and Mrs., are important. They divide the men and the women and separate the children from the adults. I'm not so sure I'd feel the same way about the Pope if everybody called him Joe, and Queen Elizabeth might lose some of her royal luster if she went by Betty. Titles help kids understand what to expect and how to behave. Just as a road sign lets the driver know what to expect and what the speed limits are, a title lets a kid know that there are limits and who's making the rules. And in our house, it's Mrs. Band.

11

Bodily Fluids

A Household Word: **Commode**

A kid who feels sick in the middle of the night, no matter how much he feels like he is going to barf, will not go directly to the bathroom. He will come to his mother's side of the bed, lean over her sleeping body and announce "I think I'm going to throw up."

Sick Sense

"I don't feel good."

My kids use this phrase like the password to paradise. I've been known to let them stay home from school, thinking that they were ill, that they needed rest, and that they were telling the truth. Ha! I am on to them at last. Here's the scam.

7am: The child is lying in bed moaning. She is too weak to rise and can barely croak, "I don't feel good." She complains that her stomach aches, her head is spinning and her throat is sore. She can't eat breakfast. She feels like she is going to throw up. It might be strep throat, Hong Kong flu or even the bubonic plague.

She seemed fine last night. So, naturally, I am suspicious and launch a basic investigation looking for a motive. Is there a math test or a social studies project due? Is the cafeteria serving something particularly gross? Does the child have gym?

If the academic calendar checks out, I examine the after-school activities. Has she neglected to practice for her 3:15 piano lesson? Are the Girl Scouts going to visit the sewage treatment plant? Finally, I scan the TV listings looking for programs that might lure her away from the halls of academia. Specials like *The Hannah Montana Marathon* are red flags.

My research yields no results and I grant permission to stay home from school. Her brothers wail in protest "No fair, we're sick too!" as I push them out the door and in the direction of the bus stop.

8am: Five minutes after the school bus drives by our house, there is a marked improvement in the patient's health. She rings the tiny bell next to her bed and requests toast. With butter. Cut into triangles. Is that a small, smug smile I detect? Maybe it's not the plague, but she still seems sick. I cancel my meetings, appointments and the child's piano lesson.

9am: She's sitting up in bed painting her toenails. "Orange juice, please," she says brightly. "With ice and a straw, the kind that bends." It looks like she's going to pull through. Maybe it's just a bug.

10am: The child feels well enough to move to the couch downstairs. She consumes two Pop Tarts and some ice cream while watching reruns of *The Brady Bunch*. Could have been indigestion.

11am: The child has changed the channel. She's off the couch and is dancing and gyrating along with Hannah Montana. They are both the picture of health.

"If I take you to school now, you'll be there in time for lunch," I suggest.

"I don't feel good," she replies.

So, instead of arguing, I've had to get tough. I'm still happy to load crackers and ginger ale on a bed tray, but you gotta be sick, really sick. And I need proof.

Fever: The most acceptable proof of illness is a temperature. The fever (anything over 99°) must be registered on a real thermometer (none of those adhesive strips) that has been placed in an appropriate orifice for the recommended length of time. Temperature readings taken without my supervision are not considered valid.

Vomiting: This is the trump card for a kid who wants to stay home. Throwing up is an all-expense-paid ticket to TV Land, no questions asked. I must, however, witness the process. Retching noises, running water and toilets flushing behind a closed bathroom door don't make the grade. Extra sympathy points are not awarded to a kid who actually vomits outside of the limits of the bathroom.

A child who says "I don't feel good," but doesn't have a temperature and isn't vomiting may indeed be sick, but I'll leave that diagnosis up to the school nurse.

EXCUUUUUSE ME!

As a mother of three, I've discovered that the position doesn't come with much power. Sure, I get to dictate bedtimes (theoretically), restrict screen time (hypothetically) and dole out snacks (continually), but the only real power I wield is with my pen. I'm not talking about this book, I'm talking about the notes I write to my children's teachers.

My excuse notes let a kid with a plantar's wart skip gym, verify that the mediocre report card made it home and grant the budding thespian permission to participate in the elementary school play. My oldest son may have his drivers' license, but he can't go to the sewage treatment plant with his high school biology class—unless I say it's okay … in writing. A note from me can create a bona fide illness out of the blahs or provide a credible alibi for a late English assignment.

Junior was unable to hand in his book report on Friday because of a family emergency.

Sincerely,

Carol Band

That's it. He's off the hook. Okay, the printer cartridge was out of ink, but in our house, that's a family emergency. I take my role of home-front correspondent seriously, maybe because I know my notes are all that stand between my kids and permanent detention.

Please excuse my child for the "stink bomb" in the lunch room yesterday. In the future, his sandwiches will contain a less pungent cheese.

Sincerely,

Mrs. Band

Sure, the power is intoxicating, but writing to a teacher is intimidating, too. I imagine my own fourth-grade teacher, Olive "Red Pen" O'Riley, as the recipient of each of my notes. She was a stickler for punctuation and she adhered to the philosophy that neatness counts. She wouldn't appreciate the notes I've scrawled on the back of last month's school lunch menu. But sometimes, in the chaos of the school-day morning, I can't find a functioning pen or a piece of paper that isn't covered with drawings of ninjas or coffee stains. More than once I've reached for my daughter's fruit-scented markers and *Hello Kitty!* stationery, which is fine for correspondence with a kindergarten teacher, but all wrong for writing to a department head at the high school.

When composing my communiqués, I fret over my penmanship and worry that the teacher will send my notes back, with red ink corrections and a sticker that says "This explains everything!" I imagine that my child's note will be sent to the school psychologist who will analyze the handwriting for genetically-trans-mitted criminal tendencies or worse, that a teacher will someday want details about our "family emergencies." That's why (on paper, at least) I try to project an inscrutable image—kind of like a combination of Mrs. Fields, Marilyn vos Savant and Dr. Quinn, Medicine Woman. You wouldn't mess with her grammar or her diagnosis.

> *Please excuse Lewis. He was out yesterday with a stomach ache.*
>
> *Sincerely,*
>
> *Carol*

Brilliant. Maybe not Pulitzer material, but to the point and legible.

"Why do you always say I had a stomach ache?" Lewis asks as he jams the note into his backpack.

"Because she can't spell hypo-chondriac," my daughter chimes in as she hands me a fistful of permission slips to sign. "I also need a note so that I can see *The Wonder of Life* in health class," she says.

I feel the familiar surge of power rush to my right hand and I grab a scented marker and write:

> *Dear Dr. Kinsey,*
>
> *My daughter has permission to view "The Wonder of Life." Although I appreci-ate the school tackling this delicate subject matter, I hope that the health cur-riculum will also touch on the considerable risks of a messy bedroom.*
>
> *Sincerely,*
>
> *Carol Band*

"Mom … can't you just write a regular note?" my daughter pleads. "This one is embarrassing."

"Just be glad I can't spell *menstruation*," I say, as I rip the final sheet off of the Hello Kitty notepad.

> *My daughter may see the movie.*
>
> *—C. Band.*

"Better?" I ask.

"Yes," she sniffs my strawberry signature and then stuffs the note into her pocket.

Whew! The power was starting to go to my head—or maybe it was just the scented markers.

READY, GET SICK, GO!

It's a fact of life—if you can call how I feel living. Moms aren't allowed to get sick. We get ten minutes to recover from a forty-eight-hour virus. Then, dead or alive, we have to get up and walk the dog at dawn, plunge the overflowing toilet and drive the kids to saxophone lessons. It's enough to make a woman take refuge at work, where at least people will tell you that you look terrible and you ought to go home.

This winter has been tough at my house. All three kids have been sick with strep throat, flu and colds. I have been a veritable Florence Nightingale, fetching popsicles, letting them watch TV in my bedroom and giving them a little bell so they can summon me if they want toast or need to throw up. I figure maybe they'll remember these small kindnesses when it's time to pick out my nursing home.

When my kids are sick, they let me know. But when my husband is sick, everybody knows. He lies on the couch in the middle of the living room and bellows like a beached sea lion. He gargles loudly and often, and threatens to move into a hotel with a health spa. The last time he had the sniffles, he put 911 on speed dial, treated himself to a bottle of thirty-year-old port (for strictly medicinal purposes) and e-mailed the producers of *Nova* with ideas for a documentary series on his cold. When I get sick, no one is interested—at least no one at my house.

"I don't feel so good," I said to my husband when I woke up this morning. "My throat is really sore and it feels like there's a bowling alley in my brain. I think I have a fever and I feel nauseated. It must be the flu."

"Nah," he said, without the slightest hint of compassion. "It's probably just that chicken thing you made for dinner last night."

"It could be the plague," I croaked.

"Does that mean you're not getting up to make coffee?" asked my loving spouse, as he looked at his watch.

"Honey," I whispered, "I just need to lie here for a few minutes—until I reach the end of the tunnel and touch the benevolent light."

"Okay, but don't take too long," he said. "It's already six-thirty and I've got an early meeting. By the way, can you pick up my dry cleaning today?"

"You don't understand," I said in a voice that sounded just like Brando in *The Godfather*. "I am sick. In fact, I might be dying. It may be just a matter of minutes before it's my turn to drive that great car pool in the sky."

I leaned back on the pillow and closed my eyes. Downstairs I could hear silverware clinking and chairs scraping. I could smell toast burning. I plumped up my pillows, smoothed my hair and waited. Surely, someone would come up with a cup of tea and some sympathy.

In seconds, there was a tentative knock at the door.

"Come in," I croaked expectantly.

It was my oldest son: "Mom, we're out of computer paper and I have to print out overdue homework."

"Use the back of last month's lunch menu, it's hanging on the fridge," I rasped in the Brando voice.

I settled back on the pillow until my daughter burst into the room. "Momsinceyouaresickandyouprobablywon'tbegoingoutatalltodayisitokayifIborrowyournewblackboots? Thanks!" she said, as she rummaged under the bed for my only decent footwear.

I was too weak to put up a fight.

She clomped down the hall in my boots and pushed past Lewis who was still in his pajamas as he approached the side of my bed. He looked concerned.

"Mom," he said. "Dad says you're sick and I'm really worried."

"Sweet boy," I thought. "This is the one who will care for me in my golden years."

He leaned in close and spoke. "Can I still have a sleepover on Friday?"

I shooed the kid away from my bed and I eyed the clock. Five more minutes until I had to pull myself together and deal with the day. I shut my eyes. Five more minutes. There was another knock on the door. My husband poked his head in.

"I was going to make you a cup of tea," he said. "But I couldn't find the tea bags, and I would have brought you toast, but I made the kids sandwiches for lunch and used the last of the bread. Lewis can't find his sneakers, the dog won't go out and Nancy called and said it's your turn to drive the kids to band practice." He looked at me with genuine concern. "Are you okay?"

My ten minutes were up. As I dragged myself out of bed, I didn't feel much better, but who knows? Maybe the folks at *Nova* will have some sympathy.

CODE YELLOW

I like to think that my children inherited all of their good traits from my end of the gene pool and all of their annoying habits from my husband's little puddle.

The way that each of my kids can raise one quizzical eyebrow, their love of Broadway show tunes and their aversion to Brussels sprouts—these fine characteristics are directly attributable to me. Their selective hearing, their messy rooms, and the way they lose their winter coats before the first snow—these are flaws that must have been passed on by my husband's faulty DNA.

Sometimes the lineage is easy to trace, like the way my mother-in-law's nose is smack in the middle of my daughter's face. Other traits are harder to identify. For instance, someone (probably on my husband's side) is responsible for my youngest son's tiny, little bladder. I figure that there must be a distant relative who missed the boat to America and got left in the Old Country because they were in the outhouse.

We didn't discover our son's condition until he was out of diapers. That's when he began repeating his mantra "I gotta go." Since then, he's spent a lot of time in the bathroom.

He has missed the thrilling conclusion of countless movies, the final inning of his Little League championship game and our family's only actual dinnertime conversation all while answering nature's call.

Because of this um … condition, I know the location of every public—and not so public—restroom in my town. I know that at the supermarket you have to go past the meat department, through the swinging metal doors, around the walk-in freezers and down a flight of stairs into the basement where a bare bulb illuminates a single seat and the walls are papered with federal safety regulations and signs admonishing the employees to wash their hands. I know where the bathrooms are in the town hall, in the branch library and in the local Greek Orthodox church. I've been behind the scenes at the firehouse, the police station and the fish market. It has been almost educational.

Together, my son and I have learned how to stride into a crowded restaurant and pretend that we are meeting friends. "Oh, I guess they're not here yet," I call out as I push him toward the washroom door.

We've even developed a code system to avert unnecessary panic. It's like the nation's terrorism alert, but we only have two colors—yellow and brown.

Last week, while we were picking up friends at the airport, Lewis announced a "Code Yellow." So we headed to the men's room.

When he was a toddler, we went to the women's room. He didn't care that the symbol on the door wore a skirt. He liked to play with the tampon machine and was happy accompanying me into a stall. Now he's at that awkward age. Too old for the ladies room and too young for me to feel comfortable sending him to the men's room alone. He is acutely aware of the difference between Men's and Women's, Guys and Dolls, Bucks and Does, and Buoys and Gulls. He says he needs privacy. That leaves me waiting—certain that he's been kidnapped by lavatory terrorists and hoping that I won't be arrested for lurking around the men's room door.

While I waited outside the airport restroom, a parade of shifty-looking characters filed in and out—old men, young men, gangsters, Hell's Angels and pro wrestlers. When the potential scenarios in my imagination began to spin out of control, I accosted a possible felon as he pushed out of the door. "Did you see a little boy in there?"

"Yeah," the felon said. "He's washing his hands."

I leaned on the door, opened it just a crack, and peeked in. I wondered if my young son knew what the urinals were and whether he could reach them.

"Lew! Are you almost done?" My voice echoed off the tile.

An old man emerged from one of the stalls. "Did you call me, sweetheart?" he inquired as he tucked his shirt into his trousers.

I apologized and let the door close. An ax murderer and an escaped convict went into the men's room. But still no sign of Lewis.

Then the door swung open and the convict strolled out, followed by my son. "Mom!" he said, jumping up and down, "the sinks turn on all by themselves!" His face was radiant. "And ... the toilets flush when you stand up!"

He is sure that I will be impressed with his discovery. But I have a discovery of my own. Maybe my son doesn't really have a tiny bladder after all. Maybe he's been exploring the physics of flushing, experimenting with hydropower and learning the mechanics of plumbing. In short, perhaps he is quenching his intellectual curiosity in the bathroom. And that's something I like to think that he inherited from me.

BRACE YOURSELF

Before we got married, my husband and I got a blood test to check for genetic glitches—like Tay Sachs and the Rh factor. We were screened for various STDs and for AIDS. The church encouraged marriage preparation classes to ensure that we were spiritually compatible, but no one ever suggested that prior to saying "I do," we consult with an orthodontist. I wish they had. Because it turns out, despite being well-matched in most areas, combining Harris' narrow jaw with my horsey teeth has had serious consequences not only for our children's class photos, but for our financial security as well.

Yesterday, that security got a little less secure, because Lewis, our youngest, got braces. My husband says that they are called braces because you have to brace yourself when you get the bill. Braces, for those of you who still have time reconsider the various ramifications of parenthood, aren't cheap. In fact, they cost thousands of dollars. It's nothing to smile about.

"His teeth don't look that bad to me," I said to the orthodontist as I squinted at my son's x-rays during the initial consultation. "Maybe we should leave them alone. A slight overbite might give him character."

"It'll give him periodontal disease,'" the orthodontist said. "Without braces, his bite will be misaligned, his bicuspids will rotate and his molars will grow through his brain. By the time he's twenty-five, the damage will be so severe that the only job he'll be able to get is as a door stop."

"Can I get invisible braces?" Lewis asked hopefully.

My immediate reaction was "No!" Call me a snob—but I figure that if I am going to shell out close to five-thousand dollars on braces, I want people to see them. I want people to look at that mouth full of metal and think, "Gee, that kid's parents really care about his teeth. They must be wonderful and generous people—fabulously successful, too.

Frankly, I don't understand how parents who seem perfectly average (and by average, I mean that they shop at Target, like me) manage to outfit a kid—sometimes two or three kids—in thousands and thousands of dollars of wires and bands. I don't understand why braces haven't become a huge status symbol—like Hummers or Hermes scarves. Why aren't there options to upgrade say, to solid gold bands or braces with a built-in IPod? I'm sure there are people who would be happy for the opportunity to spend more money, like the new parents who buy those $700 Bugaboo strollers, simply because they can. On the other hand, why hasn't some enterprising parent of genetically predisposed kids invented a cost-saving, do-it-yourself kit so you can assemble your child's braces at home using paper clips and twist ties?

When I discovered that our dental insurance would only cover a tiny portion Lewis' orthodontia, I was tempted to start bending the paper clips on my desk. I even did some research and learned that braces are a lot cheaper outside of the United States—specifically in Kyrgyzstan and Uzbekistan. Perhaps these countries might become vacation destinations for families with kids with malocclusion, the way people flock to Mexico for quickie divorces and Brazil for liposuction.

Indeed, for us the outlay of thousands of dollars for braces comes at a bad time. In our haphazard approach to family planning, we failed to consider that our youngest child's orthodontia would coincide with college tuition payments for our two oldest kids. Someone should have warned us that reproducing would mean that instead of spending our twenty-fifth wedding anniversary watching the moon shine over Waikiki, we'd be eating Kraft dinner and watching the silver sparkle in our son's mouth. Someone should have told us to move to Uzbekistan.

In the twenty-four hours that Lewis has had braces, he has been complaining that his teeth hurt, that the braces are cutting the inside of his mouth and that he is in excruciating pain. It's not often you get to lavish so much money on your kid and still come away feeling like an abusive parent. He has been mourning the list of forbidden foods (gum, mozzarella cheese, hard candy, chewy candy—all of his major food groups) and says that it still hurts too much to eat. I guess that's a good thing, because for the next two years, we won't be able to afford food anyhow.

But, when the braces come off, maybe his perfectly straight, white teeth will land him a high paying job or the lead in a Hollywood movie and he'll make millions of dollars. Then, to thank his loving parents for not letting his molars grow through his brain, maybe he'll send us on a long-overdue trip to Hawaii. Now, that would be something to smile about.

MOMSOMNIA

6:15am: *Beep, Beeep, Beeeeeeep!* Ugh. I open my left eye and squint at the alarm clock. Ugh. My mind is foggy, my head is heavy and my entire body feels weighted by fatigue. *Beeeeeep!* Only my right hand is alert. It whacks at the snooze button and successfully postpones the day for five more minutes.

Every morning I wake up exhausted. Maybe it's because I haven't really had a decent night's sleep in eighteen years. (Gee, that's how long I've had kids!) I used to think that sleep deprivation was the exclusive territory of new parents, but now, although my kids sleep through the night, I do not. Sure, I'm in bed, but I'm not getting any rest.

11pm: Brush, floss, moisturize and go to bed. Oops! My daughter's white blouse for the school concert tomorrow is in the washer. I go to the basement and put it in the dryer.

11:10pm: Return to bed. Husband is snoring. Click off the TV. Set alarm for 6:15am. Turn off the light. Close eyes.

11:14pm: Open eyes. Glare at snoring husband. I know, I know, I should be grateful to even have a husband. But he's asleep, and I'm not. Grrr.

12:36am: Eyes snap open. What was that? Maybe the cat coughed up a hairball in the dining room or perhaps a car alarm sounded on the next block. My mind races. Did I turn off the oven after dinner? I can't remember. I toss and turn and punch at my pillow.

"What's the matter?" my husband mumbles.

"Nothing," I say. "Go back to sleep." And he does.

1:47am: I elbow my husband who sleeps unaware that I am awake. REALLY AWAKE! Maybe I should stop drinking coffee. I think I read that it might cause cancer or maybe it's microwaves that cause cancer. Sometimes I microwave my coffee. I'm doomed. The world is doomed. I think about global warming and about the mercury level in tuna fish. My kids eat tuna fish. Maybe I should take them in for blood tests. When was the last time they had checkups anyhow? Have they had all their inoculations? I can't remember. I'm a terrible mother.

3:03am: *Beep!* What was that? Was I dreaming? No. Something woke me up ... **Beep!** What is that? Maybe it's the smoke alarm. No, it's not loud enough. I count the seconds between beeps: ten, eleven, twelve ... *beep!* I nudge my husband. "Something's beeping," I say. He rolls over and hides his head under the pillow.

Maybe I can ignore it, too. *Beep!* I'll just try to think of something else ... *Beep!* Arrrgh! I can't sleep! I get up to find the source of the beep and to make sure I turned off the oven.

3:06am: The beeping is coming from downstairs. *Beep!* It's the hall closet. *Beep!* It's my daughter's soccer bag. *Beep!* It's her cell phone. *BEEP!* I pick up the phone. Her friend has sent her a text message. It says, "RU Sleeping?" I turn off the phone.

3:15am: Okay, there are still three hours until I have to get up. I crawl back into bed. Ready ... I pull the covers up to my chin. Get set ... I sink into the pillow. Go! I shut my eyes and remember that I forgot to check the oven. Well, it's probably not a fire hazard. Besides, we have working smoke alarms. At least I think they work. Did I ever change the batteries? What if there was a fire? We should have a plan to escape. The kids should have rope ladders in their rooms. I wish their bedrooms were on the first floor. Why did we ever buy this house? What was I thinking? We need to move.

3:20am: Open eyes. This is silly. I should just get up. I could get a real jump on the day. I could put batteries in the smoke alarms, make appointments for the kids' checkups, cancel my daughter's cell phone service, buy rope ladders, put the house on the market, end global warming, check to see if the oven is ... zzzzzzzzzzzzzzzzz.

"Carol," my husband taps my shoulder.

"Huh?"

"You're snoring."

12

Deep End of the Gene Pool

A Household Word: **Status**

My kids always want to know which one of them is my favorite, and I say, "The one with the cleanest room."

PLAY IT AGAIN, MOM

"It's summer, do I still hafta take piano?" my son Lewis pleaded as we headed to his half-hour lesson.

"Yes," I said, thinking of the thirty dollars per week that I had prepaid through July.

"But, I hate piano," Lew whined. "And you said that if I hated it I could quit."

"I lied."

I had always hoped that my kids would be musical. And, if you walk into my house, you might think that they are. There's a saxophone under the sideboard in the dining room, an electric guitar in the den, a violin upstairs in my daughter's closet and a piano piled with mail in the living room. We've got a clarinet in the coat closet, a bass and amp in my oldest son's room and my grandfather's mandolin is hanging on the wall in the upstairs hall. Heck, you would think that we were the freaking Partridge Family.

Well, I'm no Shirley Jones, but I did hope that my kids would each play an instrument. Okay, I confess I had a few fantasies of the family gathered around the piano singing Christmas carols and harmonizing on Kingston Trio tunes, but those were short-lived. Turns out, my kids have no interest in learning a musical instrument—any instrument—and they've tried them all.

My daughter played the recorder in kindergarten. Then, in third grade, she tried the violin. In fourth grade it was flute, and in fifth grade she switched to piano. But she never practiced and, when she started hiding out at her friend's house on the afternoon of her piano lessons, we came to the mutual decision that the lessons should stop.

My oldest son took up cello in third grade, then guitar, then piano and even dabbled with an electric mandolin. Finally, he decided that what he really wanted to play was video games.

So, Lewis, the youngest, is my last hope. He too, began with recorder in kindergarten, then advanced to violin in third grade, asked to switch to saxophone in fourth grade, then quit saxophone, started guitar and then switched to electric bass. His interest in each instrument was fleeting. So, in September, I suggested that he take piano lessons. Okay, I bribed him with the promise of a new bike and told him that if he really hated it, he could quit in six months.

But he wouldn't hate it, because I found a piano teacher that was hip and cool and taught chords and improvisation and even doled out candy. This guy was everything that my childhood piano teachers weren't. There was only one thing that was the same—you still had to practice. And Lewis didn't. Oh sure, if I nagged him enough, he would sit down at the keyboard and take a stab at the chords that the cool teacher had written down. But after a minute—three minutes, tops—he'd announce "I'm done!" and make a beeline for the Xbox or the front door or the fridge.

"But I'm starving ... he'd protest. "I'm getting weak. I can't concentrate."

After a snack, he'd sit at the piano for another sixty seconds and the pattern would start again.

"I have a lot of homework to do," he'd argue. "My fingers hurt."

It was a constant struggle. His piano skills weren't improving, and all I ever did was nag.

"Your lesson is tomorrow and you haven't practiced at all!" or "No friends can come over until you practice the piano."

So it wasn't a big surprise when I drove Lewis to piano lessons yesterday and he repeated his request to quit. "I really hate it," he added.

"How could you hate it?" I reasoned with him. "You're learning all kinds of cool stuff, your teacher lets you write your own songs, he never yells ... he even gives you candy! I wish I was taking piano lessons with your teacher."

"Then do it," said Lew.

So, I took Lewis' 3:30-4pm slot on Friday afternoons. After all, I had prepaid. Now I'm learning the blues scale and some chords and even a few jazz riffs. Sure, we may never be the Partridge Family, but that doesn't mean I can't have a solo career.

THROWING IN THE TOWEL

This morning as I stepped out the shower and went to grab a towel out of the bathroom closet, I discovered that, except for the few fancy washcloths that I save for special occasions (like if Queen Elizabeth ever needs to wash up at our house), the cupboard was bare, and so was I. Wet, too. So I opened the door to the hall-way, just a crack, and yelled for someone to bring me a towel.

This was not the first time that I had been left high and not-so-dry by members of my family who seem to think that our bathroom is part of the chain of Hilton hotels—complete with an endless supply of bath towels. Again, I hollered for someone to rescue me ... no response. Why is that I can sit in my neighbor's kitchen two doors away and my kids can hear me whisper that I joined Weight Watchers, (and then share that information with the entire schoolbus stop) but they can't hear me yelling my lungs out from the second floor bathroom of our own house?

A more daring mom might have dashed naked through the hall and into her bedroom, but we are not a family that parades around the house in the buff—not since my son was two and observed "Mommy bottom BIG!" I do know parents who are comfortable walking around naked in front of their children and, while I admire their uninhibited spirit, it's not a mode that the Band family embraces. I also don't kiss my kids on the lips, although I've seen many parents plant a wet one right on their child's mouth without causing any apparent psychological damage or catching the flu, but to me it just seems ... well, icky. Perhaps, though, if we were a tad less hung up, there would still be clean towels left in the linen closet. But, we are a modest people, so I unhooked the shower curtain, wrapped it around my naked self and went to hunt for a towel. It didn't take long. On the way to the laundry room, I peered into my daughter's bedroom and spied a terry cloth heaven. Fluffy white bath towels filled the room like clouds.

Just last night, I witnessed my lovely daughter, Perry, walk from the bath-room, where she had used all of the hot water and the last of my hair conditioner, to her room. There was a towel twisted turban-style around her silken tresses, another towel wrapped around her size-zero body and a third towel gently draped over her slightly damp shoulders to ward off any possible post-shower chill. Being a teenage girl, who is actively worried about the huge negative social impact of body odor, pimples and hair that might not be as shiny as hair on Pantene commercials, it is not unusual for her to take two showers a day. Multiply that by three towels per shower and well, seventeen damp bath towels pile up quickly. No kidding. There were towels hanging on the back of her door, towels adorning her lamp, towels on the bed, towels shoved under the bed with her forty dollar t-shirts from Abercrombie and Fitch and towels that had barely touched her slightly damp shoulders and then been tossed onto her overflowing laundry hamper. I suggested to my darling daughter that while Paris Hilton, may have the luxury of unlimited bath towels, she, not being a hotel heiress, does not.

I suppose I should be grateful that she is clean—cleanliness and modesty—both very desirable qualities in a teenage girl. But seventeen bath towels? Frankly, I was surprised that we even owned seventeen bath towels. Turns out, we own twenty-eight bath towels because after I gathered the ton of terry cloth from Perry's room, I harvested seven ripe towels from my oldest son's room and three from Lewis, the youngest. Frankly, it's enough to make me want to throw in the towel, and when I do—I'll make my kids do the laundry.

HOUSE OF SPIRITS

Call me superstitious, call me crazy, but I believe in ghosts. In fact, I'm pretty sure that my house is haunted. Strange, unexplained phenomena happen here all the time.

Before we had kids, my husband and I lived in a cozy, one-bedroom apartment. Weird things never happened there. We never found Silly Putty stuffed into the bathtub drain or bungee cords hanging from the dining room chandelier. Entire boxes of popsicles never disappeared from the freezer.

There were no unexplained phenomena. Stuff stayed where we put it and the place remained relatively clean. We never found graham crackers inserted into the VCR, action figures in our bed, or the cordless phone in the freezer. It wasn't until we had three kids and moved to this house in the suburbs that such paranormal activity became commonplace.

The only explanation is ghosts. There's no other answer, because I've asked my children, "Who poured bubble bath into the toilet tank?" Nobody knows. There are no witnesses.

"What's that green stuff melted inside the microwave?" I probe. It's a mystery. No one saw anything. No one can identify a culprit. "Not me, not me, not me," they all chime.

I'm convinced that our house must be haunted. But these are not phantoms bent on evil, just mischievous spirits determined to make my life slightly more annoying.

The ghosts in our house empty the pencil sharpener and leave the shavings on the floor. They draw superheroes on the backs of phone bills and, if they can't find Scotch tape, will use a roll of thirty-seven cent stamps to hang a poster on a bedroom wall. They take the batteries out of the kitchen clock and the smoke alarms and put them into the GameBoy and the remote control car. They put my son's skateboard on the stairs and throw his brand-new sneakers into the yard when it's raining. They take my grandmother's sterling silver teaspoons and leave them in the sandbox. They hide homework assignments and notices about parent-teacher conferences. They leave lights on all over the house and download games that make my computer crash.

The ghosts are also ravenous. They'll eat the cupcakes that are slated for the PTO bake sale and drink the juice boxes that I've been saving to pack with school lunches. They eschew vegetables and leftover meatloaf, but seem to thrive on cookies and microwave popcorn.

I'm sure it's just a coincidence that the ghosts consume the same stuff that my kids like to eat. Frankly, I was surprised to learn that these spirits even had worldly needs like food. But they do, because when I ask my kids, "Who licked the frosting off the cupcakes?" all I get is guileless looks, a shrug of the shoulders and a three-part chorus of "Not me."

The ghosts are attracted to my makeup, too. I think one must be a girl, because I find my best eye pencils worn to a nub, and empty bottles of my favorite hair conditioner littering the shower stall.

The spirits must haunt the bathroom, because my teenage daughter, who spends a considerable amount of time in there, denies touching my stuff. When I ask her if she knows who broke my favorite lipstick, she shakes her silken head, bats her blackened lashes and with glossy lips says, "Not me." Must be spooks.

Lately, the spirits are wreaking havoc with the family car, too. My oldest son, who has just started driving, has convinced me that there are phantoms that wait until he's pulled into the driveway to siphon gas from the tank. He claims that it wasn't empty when he got home. The phantoms must have also reprogrammed the car radio so that now I can't find the oldies station, and I figure that they must also be responsible for the new dent in the fender.

It had to be ghosts, because when I ask my son if he might have possibly backed into a tree, he says, "Not me."

I guess we could call in an exorcist and try to rid our house of this paranormal activity. It worked for Linda Blair. But I have a feeling that if we wait a few years (maybe until the kids are in college) that these spirits might just find another haunt. You know, I'll really miss them.

LOSING IT

My kids are such losers. Every day they lose something: soccer cleats, lunch money, permission slips … shoes. How can someone lose their shoes? They lose stuff all year round, but in the winter, they are in top form. Maybe it's because there's so much more to misplace.

When my son left for school yesterday he had on a jacket (a nice one from that mail-order catalog with golden retriever puppies on the cover), gloves, a hat, boots and a backpack with his lunch and sneakers. He was carrying his violin and a plastic bag with shark teeth wrapped in tissue paper for show and tell. As he trudged to the bus stop, I waved goodbye and thought, "There's no way that all of this stuff will come back."

And it didn't. When he walked through the door at 2:45pm, he had on a short-sleeved t-shirt and goose bumps.

"Where's your jacket?" I asked with motherly concern.

"In my backpack," he replied, as he headed for the refrigerator.

"And where is your backpack?" I probed, as he stood in front of the open freezer.

"I don't know," he said, casually biting into an ice-cream sandwich. "I think I might have left it on the bus with my boots."

We drove to the school to look for his stuff. The soggy lump in the far corner of the playground was his backpack, but the jacket was gone.

So I combed through the lost-and-found box in the principal's office. None of my kids' stuff is ever there, but the sheer number of jackets, boots and even underwear is comforting. It makes me believe that my kids aren't the only ones who have problems keeping their clothes on. I checked the name tags on the Gap sweatshirts, lingered over the name-brand ski gloves and fought the urge to use the contents of the lost-and-found to completely upgrade my family's wardrobe.

In early December, I tried to thwart my children's losing streak. I bought a dozen pairs of those cheap, one-size-fits-all, little stretchy gloves. All black. I thought I was brilliant. I figured if a kid lost one glove, there would still be another to make a matching pair—and another and another and another … until they had all been left in the playground, dropped on the sidewalk, kicked under a car seat or abducted by aliens.

It took about a week for my kids to lose all twenty-four little black gloves. I call that a success, because genuine leather ski gloves and down parkas disappear even faster. I bet that you could calculate it mathematically: the value of the item divided by the wind-chill factor equals the number of days until it's lost.

I don't know what happens to all of the things that my kids lose, and it haunts me. I imagine that someday I'll discover a secret room in my house that is crammed with lost stuff. But by the time I find that room, my son will have outgrown his winter jacket.

Until then, I like to think that somewhere there's a child who's needier than mine. This winter, however, he is outfitted to the max. He's got a really nice mail-order parka, boots that have only been worn once to the school bus stop, and a dozen pairs of little black stretchy gloves.

MOB MOM

I used to worry about my kids. I thought that because they can't remember to put their shoes on in the morning before they go to school and to brush their teeth every night before they go to bed, that they were—how does one say this delicately? Average.

Now, I have come to realize that while they are standing around staring into space, not putting on their shoes, their fertile minds are occupied with really important stuff. Stuff like calculating the interest on their overdue allowance and figuring out what percentage of the cookies in the cupboard they can rightfully claim. Their memories, while selective, are very impressive. They don't remember to do their homework, but they do remember who sat in the window seat on every flight our family has taken since 1992.

They can't remember where they left their winter jackets, but they recall who got the last orange popsicle from the box that I bought last summer. They can't remember to tell me that Clive Owen called looking for a date for the Academy Awards, but they always remember when I owe them money. Although their talents might not be apparent in a traditional academic setting, I think they may have a promising future in the mob.

My oldest son forgets his lunch every day of the school year, but has a mind like a steel trap when it comes to cash—his cash.

"Mom," he said yesterday, "can I have ten dollars to go to the movies?"

"Why don't you use your own money?" I suggested. "That's what your allowance is for."

"Well," he explained with a tone of slight exasperation. "Remember last November when you couldn't pay the pizza delivery guy and I lent you seven bucks? You never paid me back. So I calculated the interest based on a five-percent annual rate, compounded it monthly and it turns out that you owe me forty-two bucks. I'll take the ten and we can call it even."

It was an offer I couldn't refuse.

Last weekend, when we had guests, Lewis, who can't remember to practice, toted his violin case into the living room. Taking his dad aside, he slapped him on each cheek and threatened: "Yo, when I was five, you promised that I would get a real allowance when I turned eight. I want it tonight. I want it retroactive from the day of my birthday party and I want it in small, unmarked bills. Hand it over or I'll play this thing. You owe me."

It's not just the boys. My daughter is also blessed with the brain of a skilled bookie.

"Hi, Honey. How was school?" I inquired as she came through the door at 2:45pm.

"I don't remember," she replied, "but can you take me to the mall?"

"Do you have any money?" I asked innocently.

"Mom," she explained with an air of limited patience. "Remember we had to take back two shirts that I got for Christmas in 2005? That's thirty dollars right there. Plus, since grandma died eight years ago she hasn't sent me any birthday money—that would be about one hundred dollars. So you owe me."

"Yeah," said the oldest son.

"Yeah," said the youngest.

"You owe us," the three wise guys chorused.

"Actually, darlings," I explained to my children, "you kids owe me. The way I figure it, I spent an average of thirteen hours in labor with each of you. Multiply that by three and add lots of interest and then compound it by three meals a day and a roof over your head. Then multiply all of that by eighteen years and divide it over the lifetime of the loan ... ahhh, just fuggedahboutit."

WAITING FOR THE MOTHERSHIP

NEWS FLASH ... Aliens are invading homes across America, inhabiting the bodies of innocent children and turning them into strange, unrecognizable creatures.

Just a few weeks ago, my charming adolescent daughter disappeared and was replaced by something new and strange; something that looks kind of like my kid only with a lot more makeup and way more attitude. Frankly, it's terrifying. It happened at my house and it could happen at yours.

Some may blame this sudden mutation on raging adolescent hormones. Others point a finger at MTV, but I know it's the plot of an alien race, intent on taking over the world, or at least creating chaos in my home. I want to believe.

Like the poster of Zac Efron that suddenly appeared tacked to her bedroom wall, the signs are everywhere. I find lotions, glosses, shadows and powders littering the bathroom vanity. I'm sure that underneath the pink blush and strawberry lip gloss there lurks a Little Gray.

Since the alien came to our house, everything has changed. My human daughter used to love macaroni and cheese, but the alien only eats organic produce—or was that last week? Tuesday she was a vegan. Wednesday she was on the South Beach Diet, and on Thursday she ate an entire pint of coffee fudge ice cream.

My Earth daughter used to think that I was pretty cool, but my outer space teen is embarrassed by everything that I do or say. She even refuses to get out of the car if I wear my flowered Capri pants and *Hello Kitty!* socks into the supermarket. I think she's worried that my behavior might call attention to her planet's plot for global domination.

Instead, she waits in the car and fiddles with the radio. I know she's not listening to a local station; she's trying to pick up signals from outside the solar system. My alien child rarely plays outside. Instead, she spends time in the house talking on her cell phone, sending text messages and typing on my computer using a language that I cannot decipher. The three letter words—brb, lol and gtg—that appear repeatedly in her communications must be some kind of interplanetary code. I think she's trying to contact the mothership.

It's also clear, from her impressive command of sophisticated electronics, that she comes from a highly advanced civilization. In fact, she is often baffled by our primitive, suburban Earth culture. Dirty dishes that have to be loaded into the dishwasher, garbage that needs to be taken out of the kitchen and emptied into trash barrels and laundry that needs to be folded and put into drawers are concepts that are far too primal for her vastly superior brain. Yet, because most of what she has gleaned about the human race comes from reading *Teen People* magazine and watching *America's Next Top Model*, she remains unclear on the concept that real Earth life requires real Earth money that can only be earned by having a real Earth job or by babysitting your real Earth brother.

Clothes are also extremely important to my teenage alien. She needs lots of really cute tops and low-rise jeans in order to effectively communicate with others of her kind. Even though her bedroom floor is carpeted with forty-dollar t-shirts from Abercrombie & Fitch, she still complains that she has nothing to wear and that I must drive her to the mall. Now! This is where she meets others of her kind to participate in pre-mating rituals and consume Orange Julius. The fate of the galaxy depends on it. The aliens know that they can bring Earth's economy to a standstill by spending lots of money at the Food Court and Sephora, which in their language means "Why pay five dollars of my parents' money for lip gloss when I can pay twenty-two dollars?"

Since my daughter turned into an alien, we have trouble communicating. I call it "War of the Words." It's obvious that the nuances of Earth English simply evade the space creatures. Just yesterday, I asked "Do you want waffles for breakfast?" and she growled "Leave me alone!" and slammed her bedroom door. Maybe I should send a text message.

If you suspect that your home has also been invaded, do not panic. I believe that these aliens come in peace and that they will be here among us only for a few more years. So, parents, hang in there and remember—we are not alone.

THE MERITS OF PARENTHOOD

A few years ago, Lewis, wanted to join the Boy Scouts and be a Tiger Cub. He was seduced by the uniform and by the merit badges. I have to admit it all sounded kind of cool in a paramilitary sort of way. But, as I signed him up to join the den, I thought "Gee, does this kid (who already had a shelf full of trophies for simply participating in soccer and blue ribbons for just showing up to T-ball) need merit badges to further boost his already inflated sense of self-esteem? It's us parents who shell out money for all these activities who deserve some recognition." When's the last time anyone gave you a medal?

I think that just like the Scouts, parents should get merit badges and wear them on a sash. That way, when a mom walked into a PTO meeting, you could sum up her achievements in a glance. Before a new mom left the maternity ward, they would be pinned with a star for the new child and a stripe for every hour of labor. As our parenting careers progressed our sashes would grow heavy with accolades. There would be merit badges for driving the carpool, for lunch preparation and for creative discipline. (Okay, son, you flushed the remote down the toilet, now you'll have change the channels manually until you are eighteen). Maybe, when people saw our crowded sashes, we'd get the respect that we deserved—or at least a little sympathy.

Maybe, if you saw a woman who had earned the *Sleep Deprivation* badge, you'd understand when she snapped at you in the supermarket checkout line. Or, if you glimpsed a guy with the *Three Kids Under Five* triple star, you'd cut him a break when he double parked in front of the video store.

The sashes would be an instant ice-breaker, too. If you met another mom at the playground or PTO, you could note that she had earned the coveted *Night on the Town* badge and find out the name of her sitter.

Just as Cub Scouts earn special patches like the *Compass Point Emblem*, parents would also garner additional recognition—maybe the Golden Pacifer—for hosting a birthday party at home on a rainy day, participating in a babysitting coop or sitting through *The Little Mermaid* more than sixteen times. Honors, equivalent to the Cub Scouts' highest level, *The Arrow of Light,* award, would be presented to parents who had survived a two-week family car trip, hosted Thanksgiving within six months of giving birth or ever volunteered to chair a PTO fundraiser. Filling out college applications, teaching your son to drive a stick shift or shopping for a prom gown with your sixteen-year old daughter are achievements that would be honored with a status akin to Eagle Scout.

The Boy Scout handbook divulges secret handshakes, signs and salutes that only scouts know. But parents also have secret information that only we possess. Take this quick quiz to confirm your eligibility in the Parent Troop.

1.   What are the names of the Teletubbies?

2.   What is the recipe for homemade play dough?

3.   What show is on your local PBS station from 5:30-6pm?

4.   Name two of the Pokemon

5.   What are your kids' shoe sizes?

6.   Fill in the blank: "Baby Beluga in the _____"

7.   Describe the location of the restrooms at your local supermarket.

Congratulations! If you are interested in becoming a member of the Parent Troop, sign-up is ongoing and meetings are held daily at coffee shops and playgrounds near you. And ... don't worry about the dues; you've already paid.

A Last Word

I used to think that after my kids were grown, my job as a mom would end. But now, after working in the business for more than twenty years, I realize that being a parent is like being a member of the Supreme Court ... or like being the Pope. It's a lifetime appointment.

Sure, that's a daunting concept, but I've also discovered that like a Supreme Court justice, you only need to worry about the federal cases. You can't sweat the small stuff—and fortunately, most of the stuff is small—even if it doesn't seem that way when your three-year old throws herself onto the floor screams *"You're NOT my mommy!"* in the middle of Whole Food's produce section.

I've also learned that, even bigger issues—like potty training and adolescence—will probably resolve themselves. As my grandmother used to say, "Nobody ever got married in diapers." Well, nobody except my Great Aunt Marion, but she married late ... very late.

It's hard to believe, especially if you've ever hosted a birthday party involving a piñata and sixteen, eight-year olds, but most kids turn out to be toilet-flushing, law-abiding, paycheck-cashing people. In fact, here are some encouraging statistics:

Of the 301,139,947 people in America, only about one million or 0.03 percent of the total population is in prison for committing a violent crime. So, the odds of your kid (or mine) becoming an ax murderer are pretty darn slim. Feel better?

Really, there's no need to thank me. You can just kiss my ring.

Carol

978-0-595-44982-8
0-595-44982-4

Printed in the United States
202050BV00002B/1-168/P